NO ORDINARY CALLING

No
Ordinary Calling

Stories of Priestly Vocation

Compiled by
Fr Stephen Langridge

ST PAULS

Cover design: Manoj Pal

First printed 2010
Reprinted 2012

ST PAULS Publishing
187 Battersea Bridge Road, London SW11 3AS, UK
www.stpaulspublishing.com

ISBN 978-0-85439-788-4

A catalogue record is available for this book from the British Library.

Set by Tukan DTP, Stubbington, Fareham, UK
Printed and bound by Intype Libra Ltd, Wimbledon, London, UK

ST PAULS is an activity of the priests and brothers
of the Society of St Paul who proclaim the Gospel
through the media of social communication

CONTENTS

FOREWORD

Priests come in all shapes and sizes!

This thought often occurs to me at the annual Chrism Mass, when all the priests of a diocese come together to renew the promises first made at their Ordination. As they process out, it is clear that no two are alike, neither in shape nor in character! Yet they are all sharing in the same ordained priesthood of Christ our Lord.

This is an important truth. It is important to the parishioners of a parish. They know that while the character, or temperament, of priests will vary, the essential ministry they bring is unchanging: the celebration of the Mass and the other sacraments and the pastoral care of the people.

It is important to the bishop, too, for he is relating not to a 'work-force' but much more to a family, with an appreciation of the distinctive strengths and weaknesses of each member.

This truth is also very important to any young man who senses that God might be calling him to the ordained priesthood. There is not a fixed blue-print for what it is to be a priest. There is no 'one-size-fits-all' model. Rather, God wants us to bring the person we are into his service, in this particular way. He wants us to be conformed to Christ without losing the distinctive, personal characteristics that make us who we are.

This truth is wonderfully illustrated in the accounts given by the contributors to this book. I am very grateful to them for their candour and generosity. I am sure their stories will encourage and inspire others, who will recognise in them something of themselves, to follow in these footsteps.

The ordained priesthood is 'no ordinary calling'. It is not an easy way of life. But it is immensely enriching and rewarding. How else could it be for it is indeed a call from the Lord who wants for each of us only what is truly best!

+Vincent Nichols
Archbishop of Westminster

INTRODUCTION

What sort of man does Jesus call to serve him as a priest? The question is an important one because many young men see such a gulf between their life and that of a priest that a vocation to the priesthood seems impossible. This book tries to answer that question through the vocation stories of ordinary priests. Here, among others, you will meet a Communist Party activist; a lapsed student; an agnostic graduate and a scientist working on the Hadron Collider in Switzerland. None of them fits a neat profile. They are ordinary men who happen to have received an extraordinary call. We shouldn't be surprised that Jesus calls ordinary men. It is how he acted in his earthly life. When he chose the apostles Jesus didn't go to the Temple in Jerusalem or to a local synagogue. He avoided the town squares where unemployed men would wait hoping someone would give them a day's labour. Instead he went to places where he knew people would be at work. Matthew was at the tax-collector's desk. Peter and his companions were fishing. If they hadn't been at work when Jesus passed by they might never have met him!

Of course when we look at our lives we are also held back because we fall a long way short of the holiness to which a priest is called. Yet in the Gospel we discover that Peter is also well-aware that he doesn't merit

Christ's trust. He falls to his knees and says, "Leave me Lord, I am a sinful man." It is precisely this humility that enables Jesus to confirm his vocation, "From now on you will be a fisher of men." Even after three years following Jesus, Peter remains a hothead and a coward. He cuts off the servant's ear. He denies the Lord three times. But he never stops trusting in God.

The stories gathered in this book are the testimonies of ordinary men. They have been repeated, in one way or another, in the vocations of countless priests down through the centuries. We have assembled them here in the hope that they may inspire us all to appreciate the great gift of priesthood. Perhaps for some young men it will be the seed of a vocation the Lord sows in their hearts.

Fr Stephen Langridge
Vocations Director
Archdiocese of Southwark

The Gift Held Out by God

Fr DOMINIC ALLAIN

Fr Dominic Allain is a Parish Priest, a School Chaplain and a Catholic writer and columnist. He was ordained priest for the Archdiocese of Southwark on the Feast of Saints Peter and Paul, 29 June 1999.

I lay face down on the cold marble floor of the sanctuary while the choir and congregation sang the Litany of the Saints. I do not really know how long for; perhaps it lasted three or four minutes, but during that time it seemed as though the whole of my life played out in front of my eyes like a film reel, one event following another at a pace just slow enough to be recognised. Watching it I seemed to see with the eyes of the heart, how everything in my life had been leading to that moment, the moment of my ordination to the priesthood. As each episode in my life was replayed it brought an indescribable sense of peace as though everything found its rightful place, everything had been a progress towards this moment, everything was included and everything was healed. St Paul says that now we see in a glass darkly, and that remains my normal daily experience of the presence of God, but in that sacred moment it was as if the light was far more than that of my own experience reflected back. It was as though a veil had lifted. I can honestly say that I have never had a moment's regret or doubt about being a priest. But for all that, the journey was not straightforward.

I am the second of five children, four boys and then a girl. My parents were devout Catholics, as were my grandparents, all of whom I was privileged to know. As the years pass the more I realise how much I am the beneficiary of their deep faith and how much 'my' vocation owes to my family and the heredity of devotion, prayers, works and sufferings that belonged to this domestic Church that formed me and was, as Pope John Paul II would say, my first seminary.

There are lots of things that signify in my early childhood but perhaps most importantly our family life was naturally shaped by the Church's calendar and her liturgy. My father was a church organist and choirmaster. From as far back as I could remember weekends and holidays were bound up with going to Mass and with the Church's feasts and I suppose from an early age I was taught to be involved in the liturgy and to take an interest in it. Even before I understood the words I was profoundly moved by the music. It was an experience of beauty and of mystery.

As well as a loving family home, I came into close contact with consecrated people. There were the nuns who taught in my primary school, and then the De La Salle brothers from when I was eight, but my parents also had priest friends and welcomed priests into our home. My father's best friend was the parish priest, an avuncular figure who gave us generous gifts and took the family out on trips. In the summer a French priest, a friend of my father's from his university days as a French Assistant in Montpellier, would come to stay with us. He was an honoured guest in our house when I was just five or six years old. I experienced priesthood as something fatherly, gentle and deeply special.

My brothers and I used to play at celebrating Mass. There was nothing flippant about this; it was all taken very seriously, we were trying to assimilate something in our play. As far back as I can remember I wanted to be a priest, just as I sometimes wanted to be an astronaut or a fireman.

This safe world collapsed one beautiful summer dawn in my thirteenth year when my father died very suddenly of a heart attack on 28 June 1975. He was forty-two years old. My mother was suddenly a thirty-six year-old widow with five children under fourteen. She turned to God for comfort, for survival, and thank God, so in my own way, did I. I remember almost rationalising it to myself that there could be no half measures; if he was the God of the resurrection then I must cling to him. The question of faith was now the real and vital one of whether love truly outlasted death, and it brought its own compelling necessity of choice. Hurled into the deep waters of faith, by a kind instinct of grace I used all my energy to strike out for something to give me support. I was a rather serious, intense, and pious teenager then. I remember I would visit the school chapel to pray at lunchtimes. At a time when others fashionably lapse I became more involved in parish life, serving on the altar and sometimes playing the organ. I loved in particular Sunday evening Benediction and the Stations of the Cross in Lent.

For all that, inside, I was in something of a turmoil. I was desperately missing my father, and a guide to the whole turbulent business of adolescence. During this time I began to attend vocations retreats at Allington Castle with the Carmelite Friars. There I first came across the Divine Office and the psalms. I remember the vivid impression Psalm 61 made on me, "Oh God you are my God, for you I long, for you my soul is thirsting." It seemed to give me great peace. I remember too, being drawn to Michel Quoist's *Prayers of Life*, with its curious titles: 'Prayer before a £5 Note', 'The Prayer of the Adolescent', Here was a new way of praying – talking to God about the things of everyday life, and listening whilst he spoke. This was something of a breakthrough in my own prayer life.

When I was sixteen and had finished my O-levels I left

home, or rather, my family moved to Norfolk and I stayed in London and got myself a job in a merchant bank in the City and rented a bedsit. Looking back it was an extraordinary thing to do. It argues for an overdose of teenage stroppiness and a kind of precocity, but also, perhaps, more positively a degree of determination and self-reliance that would one day bear fruit.

I used to commute to London Bridge Station every day, seeing the same people on the train and never speaking to them, and then I would become part of the enormous procession of people walking across London Bridge into the City just before nine every morning. After about eight or nine months of this, I had a profound experience that was like a moment of revelation, except that there were no lights or thunderclaps, just an overwhelming inner conviction. It was as if I were looking down from high above the ant-like procession of people crossing the bridge, as though I were completely detached from them. It seemed so totally meaningless and inhuman, this mass of people. I reflected that they were all going to do jobs more-or-less connected with making money, which suddenly seemed so empty, and yet presumably they all had complicated networks of people who loved them and whom they loved, as I did, and yet I would never know any of that life-enhancing aspect – I, who walked beside them every day. To all intents they were depersonalised, they were enslaved by the routine and banal; it seemed an empty sort of existence and yet I had joined the procession, was one of them; this was to be my life.

It was for a moment like staring into an abyss; feeling as though one would be overwhelmed by the apparent utter meaninglessness and loneliness of what passed for life, this progress towards death. Years later I would come across T.S. Eliot's *Wasteland*, and his own reaction to the same sight, "I had not thought death had undone so many."

Almost in the same moment there came an inner conviction of equal and opposite intensity: that God had created each of these people, that they were known and loved by him – everything about them, the very hairs on their heads were numbered – that Christ had died for them, and that being so, my relationship to them was somehow to be discovered by coming close to him who had created them and sustained them and who in the incarnation had united himself to each one of them. Again, years later I found a quotation from John Paul II, "Vocation carries the answer to the question why be a human person and how?" There was something of that question in that moment on the bridge. I came home that evening and phoned my mother and the parish priest and told them I was sure God was calling me to be a priest. It was 20 April, 1979.

I returned to Norfolk to study for A-levels; I became quite ill and for a while I was in a kind of wilderness, unable to see the future. I did, during this time, learn to love the natural world and found food for meditation in the beauty of the landscape and the seasons. It took me three years to finish my A-levels and I eventually returned to London to do so and then thought, given my state of health, it was best to go to university. I had a wonderful three years studying for an English degree. I had no other ambition than to be a priest. The question was how? Where? During university I became a regular visitor to a Benedictine Community but I knew I did not have a religious vocation. My role models were secular priests, and my experience on London Bridge had convinced me that I belonged in the world, even though my visits to the monastery were deeply nourishing experiences.

I was drawn to the figure of St Philip Neri, the sixteenth-century Apostle of Rome, and to the Oratory, which Cardinal Newman had brought to England in the nineteenth century. Here was an unusual model of secular priesthood lived in Community, and at the time I did want a Community life. In the September after I graduated I entered the Oratory and was clothed as a novice. I lasted barely six months. I was young and naïve, full of a youthful arrogance that I was going to set the world on fire, and in many ways I just didn't have the maturity necessary to cope with the challenges of this particular Community and its way of life. That was probably what made me feel as if I would have to do some kind of violence to myself if I were to stay. From this distance I can say that it was not meant to be; at the time it felt like a disaster, and if not quite the end of my hopes, certainly a massive setback.

I sort of fell into teaching – I had to get a job and it somehow seemed the obvious thing to do. One day I was a novice in an Order, the next day I was standing in front of a class of thirteen-year-olds in a prep school pretending I knew something about mathematics. It was 4 February 1988, my twenty-third birthday. One thing I do remember about that first day. It finished with the whole school going into the chapel for Benediction. The old Jesuit chaplain had compiled a very beautiful prayer book for the boys and they finished with a prayer asking for vocations to the priesthood – "We ask you to invite some of us to become priests after your own heart." To hear these young voices praying this prayer was like a balm of comfort. I felt that they gave voice to something in me. Hearing them brought a sense of peace with the conviction that if I really did have a vocation it would survive the apparent reversal it had taken.

I was to teach for the next six years. During that time I was doing my best to be open to God's will by maintaining a discipline of prayer and sacramental practice, trying to get to weekday Mass as often as I could, but I was necessarily trying to concentrate on this new career. God kept giving me nudges. The pupils would quite often say

16

things like, "Sir, did you ever think about becoming a priest?" I noticed that I felt most fulfilled when I sensed that I had made some impact on their formation as people rather than simply having delivered a narrow curriculum.

I really loved teaching and yet there was still something missing, a something that whilst teaching was fresh and diverting and I was young I could ignore, but that I knew would come back to haunt me sometime, later perhaps, at the end of my life, when I had a sense that there was something more I could have done. The 'more' was something to do with leading them to the truth. How much more beautiful and inspiring than just teaching would it be to minister Truth to these young people in the Sacraments? I was pushing thirty. It was time to settle down. The priesthood thing had never gone away and settling down somehow meant putting this to rest. I decided that I would apply for the diocese, and that I would use the selection procedure as my discernment. I would tell those charged with assessing my vocation exactly what I thought and felt, and let their answer be the definitive judgement. In the event I was indeed selected for training and so I left for the seminary with an easy heart.

I count myself blessed to have had the experience of training in Rome in the latter days of Pope John Paul II, partly because of his presence, partly because it is a city of saints and martyrs – the very stones are redolent of the story of our faith – and partly because it meant I had in some way to make a break with my former life. Some of the study was very stimulating, the community life brought a searchlight-like intensity to bear on one's own and one's companions' personal strengths and weaknesses, the routine of prayer began to take hold. There were many difficulties, but I never really doubted the direction of travel. At times of retreat during the year I found myself more and more peaceful about the vocation I had chosen. It was a question of surrendering more and more not so much to a way of life as to someone: to Jesus Christ. God, as ever, sent me wonderful role models and friends amongst the other students, a good spiritual director and wisdom and virtue in the various priests and religious with whom I came into contact. At no point in those six years did I seriously wonder whether I had done the right thing.

Of course there were difficulties, not least the death of my older brother in my third year, which again urged me to seek more deeply the face of the risen Christ. For all of this, there was no sense of having to make some huge decision as ordination neared. There was no great moment of choice, but a movement of the heart. Like the moment when I suddenly realised that I was speaking Italian without consciously translating it, in a similar way there came a point where I realised I was not constantly wondering whether or not I had a vocation. It had become part of whom I was, how I thought. Vocation is not something you put on like a garment, it is much more like gaining or losing weight; it's still absolutely you, just a little different.

I had, I suppose what some might call a very idealistic view of the priesthood. For many years, since the time I visited the Carmelites I had had one of those holy cards tucked into my breviary. It was a quotation from the great French nineteenth-century Dominican reformer Lacordaire:

> *To live in the midst of the world without desiring its pleasures; to be a member of each family, yet belong to none; to share all sufferings, to penetrate all secrets, to heal all wounds; to go from men to God and offer him their prayers, to return from God to men to bring pardon and hope; to*

have a heart of fire for charity and a heart of
bronze for chastity; to teach and to pardon,
console and bless always. My God, what a life!
And it is yours, O Priest of Jesus Christ!

Before ordination the candidate is required to make a canonical retreat. On the advice of my Spiritual Director I went, for the first time, to a monastery in France called En Calcat. Delighted with the beauty of the surroundings, I decided to explore a little and one afternoon I went for a walk to the nearest village. I went into the parish church, in a corner of which I noticed an impressive looking tomb; it was the tomb of Père Lacordaire, and a tablet on the wall quoted his lines about the priesthood. This was three days before my ordination. I took this as a clear sign that idealistic though these words may be, these were true of the priesthood, if not yet of me, and that I was indeed meant to continue to aspire to their idealism.

I was blessed to be ordained by a bishop of great spiritual stature, James Francis, Cardinal Stafford. Two weeks before my ordination he invited me to lunch. At the end of a long and wide-ranging talk he asked me how I was feeling about the forthcoming ordination. I told him I was very much looking forward to it, but that I was overwhelmed by the thought of my own unworthiness. Fixing me with a look he said emphatically, "Dominic! I will pour out the Spirit of holiness on you." And that is exactly what it felt like. That, I believe, is exactly what happened in that ceremony where I lay on the earth from which God made me and offered my life back to him; not because I am good, but because he is, and by grace transforms the creature of dust by breathing his Spirit into him to refashion him in the likeness of his Son, Jesus Christ.

The words I chose for my ordination card were, "You did not choose me, no I chose you and I commissioned you to go and bear fruit, fruit that will last." The progress to priesthood I have made to sound ordered, coherent, was none of my doing. Each stage of the journey was, in reality, part of the gift held out by God, inviting me to accept and to understand myself and all that happens to me as shaped by this mysterious choice of His love.

The Royal Navy or the Priesthood?

Mgr JOHN ARMITAGE

Mgr John Armitage is Parish Priest in the Royal Docks area of East London. He has served nine years as Vicar General of the Brentwood diocese and was previously Vocations Director and Director of the Catholic Children's Society, Brentwood. He studied for the priesthood at Oscott College and was ordained priest in 1979.

In the 1960's I attended the Vocations Exhibition at Earl's Court – it was like an ecclesiastical 'Boat Show'! The Franciscan Missionaries of Mary, who taught in my primary school in Canning Town, had an exhibition and we all went along. It was an impressive occasion, exhibitions everywhere showing us about the different types of religious life and priestly vocations within the Church.

One exhibit caught my eye: it was the White Fathers. In front of the stall was a large silver container the size of a small bucket. When I asked the priest at the stand what it was he said it was a ciborium (a container to hold the reserved Sacrament). This seemed a bit far-fetched to me because I had just learnt to serve at Mass and knew that ciboria were much smaller, they certainly were in my church. Seeing my quizzical look, he explained that because of the huge numbers of people attending Masses at certain mission stations in Africa they needed such large ciboria. I was impressed and remembered thinking to myself, "You need help." If I had to pin point the first time I thought about priesthood, it was probably then, and I was eight years old.

People don't really ask you when you first thought

of becoming a priest, but why you began on this journey. Having been asked this question many times, on reflection I realised that the greatest influence on me were the good people who surrounded me in my life as I grew up as a child and teenager. Good, not perfect – they were people who struggled with everyday life and its trials and challenges. There was a genuine goodness, that affected me greatly in my childhood and youth, and I recognise this as being the absolute foundation of my vocation as a Christian and my subsequent vocation as a priest. The example of these good ordinary people – my parents, family, priests, sisters, teachers neighbours and friends – told me something about myself, and gave me a confidence that the goodness that I saw in them was also a goodness that God had given to me.

This showed itself in a fairly dramatic way one night when I was coming home from the Sea Cadets. I got off the train and the man in front started climbing the stairs: he was obviously drunk. Halfway up the stairs he was sick and his false teeth shot out of his mouth and landed on the ground, a few feet in front of me. The words of my parish priest came to mind "If someone needs your help, then always do your best to give it." I knew what I had to do, and I walked right past them! But each step got heavier until I came back down, picked up the teeth and gave them to the man, helping him up the stairs. He thanked me and went on his way home unsteadily. As I walked home, I felt strangely good about what I had done. Later, as I reflected on that night, I realised that I could make a difference to the world in which I lived. I believe that this experience was an important step in my openness to the priesthood, because it had given me confidence in using my gifts for the good of others. Looking back at that time, it was a good feeling, but looking back on my life now I can see it was a significant moment. When we learn the joy of being a servant, especially at an early age, we begin also to understand the words of the Mass, and the example of Jesus in washing the feet of his disciples, "This is my body given for you – do this in memory of me."

I was born a Catholic and baptised at St Margaret's Church, Canning Town, in London's East End. My family have lived in the East End for many generations. Although we were a Catholic family, I cannot remember any of us ever attending Sunday Mass, but we were baptised, made our First Communion and Confession and normally attended Catholic schools. We walked in the outdoor processions and contributed to the outdoor collection (this was a weekly collection around the Catholic homes of the parish to help pay for the Catholic schools). I started attending Mass each week, I think, shortly after the Vocations Exhibition – I went on my own most weeks and enjoyed being with my friends. I could also answer a confident "Yes" when the Mass register was called on the Monday morning at school – a practice long gone in schools! I joined the choir, served at Mass and took part as fully as I could in the life of the parish. I remember nagging my mum to take me to the Easter Vigil so I could sing in the choir, and then falling asleep for the whole Mass!

As I entered my teenage years, I was involved in the parish, choir and youth clubs, and I was certainly open to the idea of the priesthood. My grandfather and father were merchant seaman and many of my family worked in the London Docks or on the river Thames. A career at sea was a strong pull for me, and I think it is fair to say that going to sea or becoming a priest were the only two real options that I contemplated as a teenager. I went to sea regularly in one form or another as an active member of Hackney Sea Cadets, and spent much of the holidays on Merchant or Royal Navy ships or establishments. I have a love for the sea and ships, that is as strong today as it was in my younger years, yet for all of my love of the sea, there was a greater pull, an awareness of an excitement at the possibility that God might be calling me to be a priest. The word excitement is a word I often use about being a priest and it sometimes surprises people as it is not a word people associate with being a priest, yet as a young man this was my strong feeling: today this is not only a feeling but a strong reality in my life after thirty years as a priest.

The Vocations Director at the time was Fr Charles Loughran and he started a vocations club called The Young Disciples. I joined and went to the monthly meetings and met other young men who were considering the priesthood. This was a great help and support as up to this point I thought I was the only person who was thinking about the priesthood and to my joy I found a group of at least twenty-five teenagers like myself struggling with the same question. One of the things that Fr Loughran used to organise were visits to various seminaries, and I really enjoyed these and was greatly inspired by the young men not much older than me who had taken the next step.

As I came to the end of my school time, I was faced with a question: the Royal Navy or the priesthood? I left school at seventeen with very modest examination results, but good enough to get into the navy, but I was too young to go forward so I worked for a year as a general dogsbody. At this time I also started to visit the seminary on a regular basis and eventually decided to apply for the diocesan priesthood.

One of the fears I faced was the thought I was not good enough to be a priest, and I was right, but I was not going to be a priest when I entered the seminary but only after six years of preparation. I wasn't good enough on 13 September 1973 when I entered, but on 16 June 1979, with the grace of the sacrament of Ordination I was given a gift by God to carry out '*in persona Christi*', in the person of Christ, his ministry to the women and men of my time and community. He knew whom he was calling, warts and all: what he needed from me was the openness to accept daily his grace to enable me to grow and change by facing the challenges each day presented.

Another fear was that it was all too big a step: how could I commit myself to such an enormous decision? How could I commit myself for life, when sometimes I could barely cope with what might happen next week? After thirty years as a priest, I have realised that there are no really big events in life, only the fear of such events. Each day God gives us the grace sufficient for that day. If we live each day and seek God's will for that moment, our fears will subside. "The imaginary trial is always unbearable, because it lacks the grace of the moment" (Maurice Zundel, *Wonder and Poverty*, Editions Paulines, 1993). The grace of the present moment is a powerful assurance that the God who calls us will give us the strength to take the necessary step, but it is only ever one step at a time.

As I look back on my years as a priest and the years of formation and discernment before I entered the seminary, I realise that the growth in my vocation can be put down to one simple phrase in the Our Father "Thy will be done". My vocation developed because as a young man I was seeking God's will and that is how I entered the seminary and after six years was ordained priest. It is the reason why I am still a priest all these years later. A vocation is a not a one-off decision, it is a life-long openness to seeking and doing God's will in the only manner possible: day by day.

My inner awareness, sometimes called a desire, was based on something real that had already happened. I desired the God who had already touched my life. If you desire God in your life it is because God is real and has made himself known to you in some way. This desire inspires the heart to great things. To follow the path of Jesus, you need to be a man of great heart, a heart open to being touched by the heart of Jesus. The desire for this "heart to heart" will give you the faith and courage to take the next step. What is that next step? To be open to seeking and doing God's will as it presents itself to you each day. It is this openness to change and growth that will be the road to finding your vocation in life.

My Lord God,
I have no idea where I am going.
I do not see the road ahead of me.
I cannot know for certain where it will end.
Nor do I really know myself,
And the fact that I think I am following your will
Does not mean that I am actually doing so.
But I believe that the desire to please you
does in fact please you.
And I hope that I have that desire
in all that I am doing.
I hope that I will never do anything
apart from this desire.
And I know that if I do this,
You will lead me by the right road

though I may know nothing about it.
Therefore will I trust you always
though I may seem lost
and in the shadow of death.
I will not fear,
you are ever with me and you will
never leave me to face my perils alone.

Fr Thomas Merton OSCO
Thoughts in Solitude, Farrar, Straus & Giroux, 1999.

Brother and Father

Fr CHAD BOULTON, OSB

Fr Chad Boulton is a monk of Ampleforth Abbey. After studying History at Cambridge and Theology at Oxford, he worked in the NHS for four years as a hospital manager. Joining Ampleforth Abbey in 1992, he was ordained in 1998, and is currently a Housemaster and School Chaplain.

It felt like an arrest, an arm on the shoulder, stopping me in my tracks. The preacher's text was familiar: "anyone who loses his life for my sake will find it". I was sixteen and my life had been focused on studies and sport at an intensely competitive school: suddenly it seemed as if I had been wearing blinkers. The preacher took the story of Naaman: "find your Jordan and jump in". It was both exciting and frightening, as though God were asking me to sign a blank cheque, without specifying what I would have to pay. All I could sense was that God might one day ask me to be a monk.

I'm still not clear where all this had come from. I had been brought up in an Anglican family. As a boy with my brothers I had served at the local parish, and then had been part of a lively, broadly-based Christian Union at my school. My family roots were Quaker and Huguenot rather than Catholic. Perhaps it was my A-level study of the medieval church, perhaps it was my parents baptising me Benedict. But thirty years on, the most convincing, and disturbing, explanation is to see this as the same call that once went out to fishermen and tax collectors. "You did not choose me. No, I chose you."

It would, however, take ten years for the blank

cheque to be cashed and for me to enter Ampleforth Abbey: in the meantime I acquired a certain reputation for angst. I certainly needed a lot of guidance in my tortuous discernment. A good friend wrote to me: "Don't worry about what you can do for God and the world. God and the world can survive perfectly well without you." My parents were remarkably patient with me. My college chaplain was an initial guide. Friends at university were wise and gentle sounding boards. After university I was part of a small community in London which met weekly to meditate on Scripture, and gave me the courage and stability to make the decision for the monastery. Throughout this process of discernment, it became clear to me that it was not 'my' vocation, but something that was only made possible by others.

In many ways my family, my education and my health had provided a very privileged start in life and the classic recipe for middle-class guilt. A priest at university told me "Don't feel guilty, just be generous." Growing up in 1970s London, however, had not been an upbeat experience: the glass seemed half empty, a society with decreasing joy, hope and trust. At best, like Benedict, I felt the need to return to the source, to find the springs that could renew. At worst, like Jonah, I felt the impulse to run away and hide. But even here, like Jonah, I discovered the relentlessness of God's mercy. Paul was right to glory in his weaknesses: they do become the avenues of grace.

I was not an unhappy Anglican. It was more that I was attracted by the Catholics I met. A university ARCIC discussion group proved a bridge, a way in to understanding previously alien terminology. A Catholic seminarian on placement at an Anglican theological college provided challenging discussions. Visits to

Downside Abbey introduced me to the Benedictine tradition of prayer. Degrees in history and then theology enabled me to study Catholicism in theory and in practice. My history supervisor opened my eyes to the nature of the Church through study of the Reformation. I began instruction under the Catholic chaplain, but encountered such opposition to 'swapping spiritual bank accounts' that I decided to wait, to check that this was more than a university fad.

I ran away from religion, headed off to the far end of the country and got a job in hospital administration in Carlisle. This was a time of blind, sometimes desperate, prayer: "your will be done", repeated amidst the diversions and distractions of life for a twenty-something, that intensified when I moved to London. My prayers seemed like dots placed on a page, seemingly random at the time, only in retrospect revealing the shape and curve of a vocation. Finally, in 1991, I made a first decision and headed up to Ampleforth. Creeping to the Cross on Good Friday roused the ancestral voices within to one final challenge but, after twenty-four hours of turbulence, I was received into the Catholic Church at the Easter vigil. I never felt that I was required to deny my Anglican upbringing, to which I owed the foundations of my faith. A vocation is never from scratch and I always felt that I was bringing my Anglican inheritance with me.

A second decision now confronted me. On a grey Saturday in January the following year, saying evening prayer in my South London bedsit, I saw clearly that I had one life to lead and that seeking God mattered more than the career and marriage I was still looking to establish. A good friend had warned me that if I couldn't live like a monk in London, it wouldn't be any easier at

Ampleforth. So I sold my car, slept on the floor, went to daily Mass and said the Office on the bus to and from work. I slipped into a local church at lunchtime each day simply to spend five minutes in silence. Three months later, after talking things through with my parents, I gave in my notice at work.

In joining a Community that was busily pastoral rather than strictly contemplative, I was attracted by the combination of a monastic and a priestly vocation and it is difficult in this account to separate the two. The monastic profession of vows is the primary step: you are a monk first, a "brother", and you may then ask to be ordained a priest, a "father", as a secondary step. But inevitably my discernment of whether to stay in the Community concerned my future both as a monk and a priest. I can remember in the novitiate, during the feast of the Sacred Heart, saying "Of course you can have my heart, but why here?" and then hearing "Do you think it is a co-incidence that you can give your heart here?" After a year as a novice, I took temporary vows for three years, at the end of which I was free either to take permanent vows, or to leave. I nearly left, feeling that the 'magic' had gone and making plans for a new future. Standing at the door of the monastery, however, I found that there still remained outside me a call to stay, even though there was no desire within. It was a strange way to discover that my vocation was not dependent on my feelings: "Not my will but yours be done."

Two years later I was ordained a priest. Because I already had a theology degree, my training was completed in the monastery, with a combination of monks, visiting tutors, and for one year a fortnightly trip to the Dominicans at Edinburgh to work my way through the Summa. It was not the traditional seminary formation, but I learnt most from being part of a Community of priests. The Ordination itself was a day of extraordinary happiness – my younger brother was even moved to propose to his girlfriend immediately afterwards. Six of us were ordained priest by Cardinal Hume, in the year before he died. At the point where the priests laid their hands on me, all I could see with my head bowed was a succession of anonymous shoes going past, as though the gift being passed on was independent of any particular personality. I can still remember the overwhelming sense of affirmation when first the Cardinal and then a succession of family, friends and brethren all knelt down asking for my blessing.

The reality since then, of course, has not maintained that level of intensity. Once the various steps of monastic profession and priestly ordination are over, there is the almost unavoidable sense of a plateau. Priesthood in a monastery is often a latent gift, exercised when opportunities arise. For several years, I ran a small group for young men and women discerning their vocations. Within the school run by our monastery, I am a Housemaster and now School Chaplain. Perhaps my strongest experience to date has been the annual pilgrimage to Lourdes, where being a priest seems the most natural of roles. On the other hand, when travelling elsewhere, I have encountered suspicion and even hostility. Once, wearing my habit in London, I was spat at by a passing motorist. More often the sight of my clerical collar seems to produce in others an uncertain response, as though something unfamiliar and threatening has just come across their radar. In this light, it is a sort of peculiar freedom to know that priesthood enjoys no privileges, that the Church is confronted by a time of testing that will either be simply humiliating, as it loses its wider cultural supports, or will be truly humbling, as it re-discovers its deeper spiritual roots.

There are dangers, however, in drawing any general lessons after just twelve years as a priest. This account is inevitably provisional, a sort of stock-take. There will be plenty of testing times to come. I'm aware that my story lacks a grand sweep, and in particular any clearer sense of the Church's social mission. I was not brought up in a Catholic parish, and I have not, yet, served in a Catholic parish. Monasticism can become the private faith of co-habiting spiritual bachelors. But God invites us as we are, to give what we can: Paul VI called for witnesses, not teachers, and the vocation of a monk-priest is to be a faithful witness to the Gospel by living out the Benedictine Rule. Learning how to love is perhaps the greatest challenge. I remember a senior monk telling me in my novitiate: "Virginity is a fact, chastity is a norm, but celibacy is an art." The original Cistercians understood the art of loving. Bernard of Clairvaux saw love as water, "a wonderful thing, provided it always returns to its source, from where it can pour forth with renewed energy." Aelred of Rievaulx saw love as fire, "the divine fire, that absorbs as though they were mere sparks the other human loves."

The strong moments are when the water flows and the fire burns, when as a priest you are invited into people's lives and when as a priest you are available to honour that trust. There is something freeing about the sacramental role of a priest: you have something to do, something to offer, a role rather than just a presence. There have been more than enough regrets, infidelities, negligences, shortcuts. But stronger still than this is a recurring sense of God's mercy, and a surprisingly unshakeable sense of God's choice. Before my first homily, an older priest advised me to ask: "Am I preaching myself or am I preaching Christ?" The mystery of this vocation is that ultimately it is not about my performance and not in my control. John XXIII would remind himself each night: "Remember, Angelo, you're not running this show." I once gave a beautifully crafted talk to some junior monks, at the end of which one of them leant back and remarked: "That would make a good Christmas sketch!" On the other hand, I have received letters of thanks for advice and comments I can't even remember.

It is an extraordinary way of life, lived out in the very ordinary day-to-day. I suspect young men shy away from the priesthood because they are anxious about its demands and jealous of their freedom. What helped me to join the monastery was this counsel from Rahner: "There is no human freedom without decision – a man who wants everything never makes a choice and never really gets hold of anything." I wonder today whether we are so concerned to keep our options open that we never exercise them. We are afraid of failing so we avoid commitment. That was certainly why it took me so long to make a final decision. What matters is what we are free for, rather than what we are free from, something the psalmist understood. "I will run the way of your commands; you give freedom to my heart."

Gift and Mystery

Fr AUGUSTINE CONNER, CFR

Fr Augustine Mary Conner is a member of the Community of the Franciscan Friars of the Renewal. He was ordained priest on 12 May 2007 at St Patrick's Cathedral, New York.

I remember sitting in a pub at the age of fifteen, with some of my school friends. We were enjoying a furtive pint and talking about our futures when, plucking up some courage, I interjected "Don't you think that God has some special plan for your life?" My friends looked at me for a moment and quickly dismissed my question with a resounding "No". I think it was probably at that point in my teenage years that I also tried to dismiss the idea from my immediate consciousness and really did not expect the question to surface again. Yet, I had always felt that I existed for a reason. I could not explain why I felt that way. Maybe it was because my parents had helped form within me such an idea or maybe because deep down my heart just knew it.

I first thought of wanting to be a priest at the age of six, a little before I made my First Holy Communion. I liked the priest in our parish and enjoyed serving at Mass. And also among the games I used to play at home was 'the Mass'. I knew the words of the Mass by heart and putting a towel around my shoulders used to 'celebrate' it with liturgical proficiency. I would say that Jesus was very real to me and I close to him. Admittedly, as I entered my late teens, however, he became very far from my thoughts as I lost myself for a while in our hedonistic culture.

As I came to the end of my second year at Nottingham University where I was 'studying' Ancient History I became very aware how empty I was. I was going to Mass occasionally but it was not making much of a difference to my life. Then, during the summer holidays of that year in August 1997, my aunt offered to pay for me to go away to a youth festival in Medjugorje with one of my brothers, my sister and three cousins. I was, of course, open to a holiday in the sun with forty thousand young people from around the world and the fact that it was a "big retreat" did not put me off. I had no idea or expectation that it would have any serious impact on me. Little did I know that that week would change my life for good.

One of the first things I noticed at the festival was how joyful the other young people were. I had not seen joy like that before. I had seen attempts at joy and happiness in pubs and nightclubs but nothing that came close to the authentic joy that was all around me. I knew I wanted that deep joy. And so I went to Confession. I had been the year before in St Peter's Basilica while on holiday in Italy, but I had not made an integral Confession because I was not, at that point, willing to change the direction of my life. Now, however, I was ready to start again. I thought that if I just confessed my sins as quickly as possible the priest would give me absolution and, with as little discomfort as possible, I could get back on track with God and continue on my journey.

The priest who heard my Confession was a little Irishman. He not only heard my Confession but he helped me make a full Confession. He gave me absolution but I am sure he had absolutely no idea what happened in my soul. I felt a heavy darkness lift from me and I was filled with a joy that I had never experienced before. Up to that point I had hoped that God existed, but now I knew he did. Everything became clear for the first time in my life and as I stepped out of the confessional I looked up and said "Ah, so do you want me to be a priest?"

I was so happy. I was drunk with happiness! I had experienced Jesus through that Confession in a way that I did not think possible.

Life could not be the same. I had met God in such a way that I felt I had to respond to his love as completely as I could. I began to pray and prayer came naturally from the heart. The Scriptures became my rule and the Eucharist became my strength. I went back to university, however, with a lot of fear because I knew that I had to change my way of life and I knew that I would have absolutely no support. It was very difficult but by the end of my last year I was going to daily Mass, Confession at least once a week and was praying an hour or two each day. Meanwhile the idea of priesthood was growing within me.

The following summer I decided to go back to Medjugorje for the youth festival to ask Our Lady for clarity in my discernment. Whilst there I gave her an ultimatum. I prayed on one of the days "If tomorrow at Mass the priest says, 'Put your hand up if you think you may have a vocation to the priesthood', I'll do it!" Well, to my great surprise that is exactly what happened! And he not only told us to stand up but to come to the front of the church to be prayed over. Our Lady had answered my prayer and so I felt I was bound to take the 'call' seriously. The following month, therefore, I went to a Youth 2000 retreat at Worth Abbey. It was my first experience of Youth 2000 and I loved it. I felt very much at home there and during the middle of the night when I was in Eucharistic Adoration I made a deal with Jesus. I said to him, "I'll be a priest if you give me a Community." I knew how tough it was to live in the world as a committed Christian without support and I knew that I would not be able to be a priest without the support of other priests and brothers who were striving for holiness.

I knew absolutely nothing about religious life. Whilst I was at that retreat, however, I picked up all the vocational information I could get my hands on. I was struck most by the vocational information about the Franciscan Friars of the Renewal. I knew nothing about St Francis but in the pictures of the friars I saw young men who looked happy. They wore habits, Eucharistic Adoration was part of their daily life, they loved Our Lady, they loved the Pope and the Church and I was struck by their work with the poor. The only problem was that, at that time, they only had friars in the Bronx and I had absolutely no desire to go to America! However, I had heard some Englishmen had joined them so that made it a real option.

I visited the Friars in New York because the doors seemed to open in that direction and I loved it! I loved it so much they said I could join the following year if I wanted. It seemed like the right thing to do, and so I did. I was twenty-two years old when I joined. However, I would be lying if I were to say it was easy. From the moment I joined, I struggled. The first year-and-a-half was particularly difficult. Getting used to the daily routine of our religious life: the early mornings, the late nights, living in Community, a different culture, the lack of freedom, and living in the Bronx and Harlem was very tough. I think, without doubt, I would have left if I had not had such a clear sense that I was where Jesus wanted me to be. I had to trust him a lot. Even so, I would not get out of my head the prophet Jeremiah's words "You dumped me, O Lord, and I allowed myself to be dumped."

Jesus' own words, on the other hand, gave me strength "You did not choose me. No, I chose you." Indeed, these words sum up my sense of my vocation. I came to realise that the call to the priesthood and religious life is his work. He calls someone to himself and asks him to freely surrender everything to him. He not only asks for his material goods but all that he is and all the gifts he has to give: he asks for everything. I am amazed at what he asks and yet only he could ask because he alone gives everything. He gave everything on the Cross and he gives all that he is in the Eucharist. Over the last ten years, then, I have tried to respond and to accept his call, which constantly challenges me to surrender. And yet, when I look back I can see clearly how his grace has transformed me and, indeed, continues to transform me to make me more like himself.

I was ordained priest by the Archbishop of New York in St Patrick's Cathedral after being a friar for seven years. It was such an amazing day. In fact, it was so overwhelming that I can hardly remember any of it! Actually, it took me at least six months for my feet to finally hit the ground. I had such a longing to be a priest before Ordination (that longing, and all the football and squash I played, were the only things that helped me persevere through seminary) and yet, I have to say, that I still have such a longing to be a priest. I love being a priest! I feel that at last I am beginning to live the life that I was created to live. However, by that I do not in the slightest mean that I am finally and definitively fulfilled. I know that will only happen when I am in heaven.

I did not feel any sense of being infused by the Holy Spirit at my Ordination. In fact, I did not feel anything at all inside. Indeed, as a priest I am generally unaware of the Lord's presence working in or through me. That is not to say, however, that I do not believe that he has been and remains very active through the gift of the priesthood. What I realised very quickly, though, is that to all appearances I am exactly the same person and that is the wonder of this sacrament. Christ shares his priesthood, configuring a man to himself in the depths of his soul, without disturbing the integrity of the man. Thus, the priest has to spend his whole life allowing himself to be continually transformed by the working of the Holy Spirit so that the distance between Christ and himself becomes less and less. So that one day he may be able to say, "I live not I but Christ lives in me." This is, I am convinced, what the priest is called to by virtue of the sacrament of Holy Orders. Like every Christian, but to a greater degree, he is to become *alter Christus,* 'another Christ'. It is not enough, therefore, for a priest to simply administer the sacraments and in every way to live a 'normal' life. The fruitfulness of his ministry and indeed, the fulfilment of his personality depends on him conforming himself to Christ.

As a religious, my experience of the priesthood is quite different from the experience of the average diocesan priest. Our share of the priesthood of Christ is, of course, equal but, since the priestly vocation is lived within a particular context (either within the diocesan framework or within a particular religious order), it is experienced differently. For example, the priesthood within our Franciscan Community is lived outside the setting of a parish. It is lived within the context of our charism and mission, which is fundamentally rooted in a life of prayer, a common life, service to the poor and evangelisation. That is not to say that we do not work very closely with parish priests, and we always work in communion with the local diocesan bishop, but it does mean that we are free to exercise our priestly ministry beyond our immediate location. The result is that we are often invited to preach and to celebrate the sacraments all over the country, and even abroad, in parishes and at retreats. My experience therefore as a Franciscan priest, when I am not in the friary, is very missionary and very diverse.

In conclusion, I would like to mention something St Padre Pio, a model Franciscan priest, once said: "I am a mystery to myself." He was, of course, speaking primarily of his life and vocation as a priest. He understood clearly that the priesthood is a divine mystery and the vocation to the priesthood is so far beyond the person called. Sometimes we think our response to our vocation is all about us, but it is not. It is all about God's initiative. Before the world was created he chose us in Christ and, for those called to the priesthood, he planned for all eternity that we would share in his Son's priesthood. In fact, this is why we were created! It is for this reason that the person called to be a priest discovers his deepest identity when he responds to his vocation with generosity and without fear. I have discovered this myself and, though quite aware of my potential capacity for infidelity and my innate weakness, I can say truthfully that it is my greatest joy to be a priest!

Leap of Faith

Fr PHILIP CONNER

Fr Philip Conner is the Youth Chaplain, Diocese of Lancaster. He was ordained priest on 12 November 2005 at St Maria Goretti's, Preston.

It was another lazy breakfast. My brother sat opposite me and had been reading a leaflet on the Franciscan Friars of the Renewal, which he had picked up at a recent retreat. I was still in a state of mild shock that he had been on a retreat in the first place but when he leant over and said, "What do you think about me joining these friars?", I choked and a mouthful of cornflakes flew across the table in his direction. I couldn't believe what I was hearing. It wasn't just the thought that my brother might seriously be pondering a vocation, but the fact that I too had just arrived at the same point, thinking that God might be calling me to be a priest. Two vocations in a family, I thought, this is impossible! But I was soon to begin to understand that nothing is impossible to God.

From my youngest age I have loved the mountains. I was brought up to play in streams and rivers and to climb hills and to camp under the stars. Through school and university, the wild places lured me like nothing else. Climbing in the Alps, I remember one occasion setting off from our glacier base-camp just before midnight. We climbed through the night under the moonlight which cast its deep shadows over the rivers of ice, and we reached the crest of the mountain just as the sun was rising. All day we walked on very limited reserves – jelly cubes and marzipan, I seem to remember, toiling onwards with crampons, ice-axe and ropes. By the end of the day, tiredness had set in and a misreading of the map led to us coming down a gully we should never have descended. Steeper and steeper it became and there seemed no way out. Pitch by pitch I was let down on the rope. Towards the bottom, a wide crevasse yawned before us, the only thing standing now between the mountains and freedom beneath. Tired from the day's walking and seeing no alternative, I decided that I would jump the crevasse. With great aplomb, I leapt above the unknown, only to lose my footing on the last step and plunge into oblivion. As I hung upside down in the darkness, I prayed like nothing before. "Yes, Lord! I will be a priest if you really want me to be. Just get me out of here!" Sure enough the Lord got me out of that tight situation and on this occasion I lived to tell the tale.

Though this would make for a quick explanation of how I came to be a priest, the Lord is much more subtle and the real reason for becoming a priest is a bit more complicated. The Lord, however, didn't lose the opportunity to teach me an important lesson. Whilst I was rescued from the jaws of death, I had accidently left the top pocket of my rucksack open, and in all the confusion of the moment hanging upside-down in the crevasse, the contents of this pocket emptied themselves… all our money, tickets, passport. Little did I know that the adventure was only beginning. For a few days we sat on the side of a road waiting for some friends to pick us up, and when they did not appear, I had the idea that we should hitch-hike to a friend's house near Geneva. It was a further two days later that we arrived in Geneva only to find out that the friend I thought was there was on a family holiday. Four days without any food, sleeping rough on the streets of strange towns after two weeks of mountaineering, left me feeling pretty weak and wretched. As I reflected upon this experience of hunger and destitution, I felt the Lord saying to me: if this is what happens to the body after four days without any food and shelter, what happens to the soul when it is neglected? What happens when we forget the One who made us, when we no longer know his love, when we lose the taste for life through our sin? This was a stark wake-up call for me as I began to understand that I could no longer live my life for myself. For the first time I began to understand the emptiness within me, an emptiness that nothing could satisfy but God and I began to thirst.

Something inside me had been thirsting for more from life for a long time. The mountains, the wilderness, the stars I had so often gazed upon, had always reminded me that there was something more out there: their beauty had always inspired me. If this was what God can create, how much more beautiful I thought must this God be. And then came the insight – if this creation was beautiful, how much more beautiful was each person, made in the image and likeness of God? I found myself lost in wonder as I began to contemplate how everything in creation is passing, but we – human beings – are made for eternity to share the life of God, and that we can begin to live that eternity now – in and through love, in and through the One who is Love. As a young man in my early twenties, this truth was something utterly captivating.

I had always experienced the love of God through my family – my beautiful Mum and Dad whose devotion to my brothers and sister and to me, and whose love for one another and faithfulness to the Lord ran through everything. Perhaps it was the natural soil in which a vocation to the priesthood might be expected to flourish. But there was something more mysterious here. Though I had an inclination to be a priest from my early teens, I began to understand that it was something much more than this, that it was in fact a divine gift. Whilst many times through my teens I experienced God near to me, often I would end up either ignoring him, taking him for granted, or worst of all, refusing to place my trust in him and what he was calling me to. On one level, I never stopped drawing close to the Lord, attending Mass and making time for prayer all the way through school and university, but on another level I began to live a life at odds with what I believed though, at the time, I rarely allowed myself to see any contradiction. But all the time this thirst began to emerge deep within me, that desire for authentic love, for authentic meaning – and I felt so empty without it.

Finally I found myself on a pilgrimage to Medjugorje in August 1997 and I thought I should go to Confession as that was the sort of thing one did on pilgrimage. Not preparing myself particularly well, I walked past all the confessionals offering Confession in English and went into a booth with an Italian priest who spoke very little English. "Great!" I thought. But as I went through my usual list of felonies in a half-hearted fashion, the priest looked at me deeply and with the few words of English that he did speak – inspired by the Holy Spirit – he put his finger on deep wounds within me and helped me to understand the truth of God's love and mercy. My life would never be the same again. He prayed with me and for me and gave me absolution. I stood up, thanked the priest and opened the door to a wholly new life. Words will never express what happened on that day; my life was transformed and I was touched to my very depths by the amazing power of God's mercy, his love for me, the gift of the Holy Spirit. I was free.

Something amazing began to happen in my life from this point. From harbouring a vague notion of being a priest, the desire in my heart now grew for holiness – I just wanted to be with the Lord. The love the Lord showed me was so deep and so transforming, I wanted nothing but to give myself to him. But how? I felt the Lord calling me to go to a quiet place and to learn how to listen to him, and to depend upon him.

As it happened it was at this point in my life that I was due to leave St Andrews University in Scotland and spend a year researching in the small provincial town of Montauban in southern France. This could have been a terrifying year, away from all my family and friends in a country whose language I had barely mastered, living by myself. But far from being a lonely time, it was a year of great richness. It was the year that I began to experience a lot of healing, a renewed inner life, and a desire to do the Lord's will – and a burning love for the Real Presence in the Eucharist. It was the year I began to love Our Lady in a new way. She had been the one who had cajoled me onto the summer's pilgrimage on which everything had changed and now – in her ever practical manner – she taught me how to unite myself to her response to the angel Gabriel, "Be it done to me according to your word." For a long time, I had lived in fear, never putting a foot out before I knew where it would land, always playing things safely and in a way that I was able to control. Now that could no longer be the case. Mary taught me what it meant to wait, what it meant to prepare myself for the Word of the Lord and I had a great sense of her comfort and care burning away my fears.

When I returned to Scotland after the year I knew I faced testing times. I realised my life had changed and could not continue as it had done so before I left for France and I wondered how this would affect the relationships with my existing friends. I need not have feared. Far from limiting me, I discovered a freedom that comes from becoming more truly myself.

My aunt – another important figure in my life – had always taught me to search for the places of life in the Church and to draw from them. Whilst many bemoan the decline of the Church's influence, particularly in the West, those seeking Christ will find him – as in every age – in surprising places and in remarkable ways. I know I have been spoilt to come across so many beautiful people who have responded to the grace in their lives and so many different groups and movements and religious orders that have fed me spiritually. Time and time again I found myself coming across other young people at Youth 2000 retreats, at World Youth Days, in the different French Communities that I came to know, who shared my thirst for Truth and for life and for love, and who showed me that it is possible to live the faith today, and more than that: who showed me that this is a time of many great graces.

I remember one occasion battling across Paris to get to a church run by the Emmanuel Community for an evening Mass after work one day in the summer of 1999. As I knelt before the Blessed Sacrament, and after many years of waiting, I heard the Lord prompt me in as clear a voice as I have ever heard, "It is time. Write to the bishop." Strange as it may sound, up until that moment, I had never thought of the diocesan priesthood.

I had always been thinking in terms of religious life – never knowing which religious order I was called to, all with their wonderful charisms. But now I sensed that there was something specific to the diocesan priesthood, that the Lord was calling me to this – though I little understood it.

I have to say that the journey to the priesthood through the initial discernment and then seminary and now as a priest has never been an easy or straightforward one for me. But I always understood that if God was calling me he would give me the grace to respond and to live this out. So there was no need for fear. And yet I was afraid. I remember on the day of my Ordination, pacing around the presbytery kitchen, praying my Rosary, glancing towards a framed picture of John Paul II, the Pope who was forever exhorting us not to be afraid. At that moment, I remembered the words of Jesus to Peter on the shores of Galilee after all the betrayal and dereliction of the Cross: "Do you love me?" With Peter, I responded, "Of course I do", and every time I did so, my fears melted away like snow in the sunshine. All fears melt away in the face of this conversation. How can I not love the One who gave everything for me? As I entered the church and heard the singing and the prayers, and as I lay on the floor as the Litany of Saints was sung, as I stood before the bishop surrounded by all those whom I loved and who I knew loved me, I felt in myself a desire to give everything. For the first time in my life, I let go into love, a love that never ceases to unfold in strange and marvellous ways.

The Longest Journey

Fr GARETH LEYSHON

The Rev Dr Gareth Leyshon was appointed to the Pontypridd Deanery Team Ministry as a deacon in October 2006, residing at St Dyfrig's, Treforest, and was additionally appointed a member of the Ecumenical Chaplaincy to the University of Glamorgan in February 2007. He was ordained a priest of the Archdiocese of Cardiff, in St Dyfrig's, by Archbishop Peter Smith on 5 May 2007. He is currently priest-in-charge of St Dyfrig's and retains his University duties.

Picture the scene. It is August, 1993, and I am sitting by a riverbank in Kent. Soon I will begin the final year of my Physics degree at Oxford... and then what will happen? I'm male. I'm single. I'm a Catholic, and have been for the last three years. I wonder what God might want me to do with my life next? I could always ask him... but what if he were to ask me to try the priest thing? No. I don't want that. Anything but that.

The river in question is the Medway. I'm at Aylesford, the Carmelite friary, for one of the first big youth festivals organised by the fledgling Youth 2000 organisation in England. My being here has a lot to do with a pretty girl. After all, few things would be more un-Gareth-like than to travel to a strange place, serving food over which I (then, a fussy eater) have no control, and having to sleep, for the first time in my life, in a tent! Last year, the pretty girl persuaded me to come and visit the festival for a day. I rather liked what I saw... there was all-day Adoration of the Blessed Sacrament, and daily Rosary. I'd become a Catholic because I believed that when Jesus said, "This is my body", he meant it, and I rejoiced in the idea that the saints in heaven have a special role in praying for us on earth.

So, a year on, here I am, accompanied by the Real Presence of Christ, ambient devotion to the Blessed Mother… but no pretty girl, whose heart had led her in another direction. My heart had been so drawn by the Catholic faith evident in this festival, that I had come and was willing to risk camping conditions, even without romantic motives. And now I had a decision to make. Was I willing to put my trust, without reservation, in Jesus? I wasn't even clear why I felt this inner resistance to the very possibility of priesthood, but there it was. As I sat on the riverbank, the sheer inexorable logic of the situation dawned on me. If Jesus was who I believed he was – God made flesh; if he loved me enough to die for me; and if he was the one person I would willingly call Lord, then I had no business telling him what he wasn't allowed to ask me to do. "OK Lord," I prayed. "You win. Tell me what you want me to do after this degree and I'll do it – even if it is the priest thing."

In the short term, it wasn't the priest thing. I cautiously explored the idea with my chaplains at Oxford, who suggested I was still a very young Catholic and needed time to grow. I applied for Physics PhD places, but was turned down everywhere. Just when the way forward seemed as clear as mud, though, an unexpected offer dropped through the letterbox: "Assistant Chaplain wanted: no experience necessary." Nottingham University sought a lay assistant, a recent graduate, to work with its priest-chaplain, and much to my own surprise, September 1994 found me working for the Church in Nottingham.

My Nottingham year wasn't easy. My own heart was hungering for prayer groups, for spreading devotion to the Blessed Sacrament, and to Our Lady. The Catholic students at Nottingham were passionately committed to various social justice initiatives. In that one academic year I made every pastoral mistake in the book and a few that haven't appeared in print yet. By the end of the year, I had learned the hard way about the importance of beginning with other people "where they are at" – and the Nottingham students had started a prayer group!

Meanwhile, I was head-hunted. Cardiff University, which had passed over my application for a PhD in 1994, wrote unexpectedly to offer me a place, with government funding, for the following September – please reply by 6 January, 1995.

To go, or not? By now, I was committed to taking these important questions to prayer, and asking Christ what he wanted for me. But prayer throughout December yielded no clear sense of YES or NO. My parents found me in a melancholy mood that Christmas. Wasn't saying "YES" to this offer a no-brainer? What was I waiting for? They didn't understand my need to know what God's opinion was.

New Year's Day 1995 found me at another Youth 2000 event. I'd spent the last few days begging God for clarity, to no avail. I'd been up until 3 a.m. for the Midnight Mass and New Year party. After a little sleep, I rose for prayer – I'd volunteered for the 6 a.m. shift in the all-night Adoration, and spent another hour begging God for clarity. None came. Neither did the 7 a.m. relief person. By 8.30 a.m. I had spent the best part of three hours praying on my own before the Blessed Sacrament – and still no sense of the right decision. But that same evening I walked into the chapel, and the answer hit me like a ton of bricks. In another moment of inexorable clarity, God seemed to remind me that last year, travelling straight from a retreat to a science festival had provided a natural opportunity to share faith with a scientist friend, who had subsequently taken a step closer to God. In the same way, I was now to step back from full-time Church work to the world of science, to be a witness. I had my answer, and generously, with four days to spare! (I've come to appreciate that God's usual approach to deadlines is either to answer prayer at the eleventh hour, or to wait until the thirteenth while arranging for the deadline to move!)

In September 1995 I moved to Cardiff, where I spent three very happy years. My day job was researching dust in distant galaxies. In the evenings, I devoted my time to helping develop the activities of Youth 2000 (becoming regional leader of the South Wales & South West group) and of Catholic Charismatic Renewal (becoming secretary of the new Cardiff team). Through these two roles, I met and worked with many priests of the Cardiff Archdiocese.

By January 1997, it was time to ask the Big Question again – "Lord, what next, when I finish this doctorate?" I had no great urgency in praying around the question when I went on the 1996/97 New Year retreat, but I was still in London on Saturday, 4 January, when Youth 2000 held a day of prayer in Kensington. That day's speaker was a Franciscan Friar of the Renewal from New York, and he spoke at length on vocation – and on the importance of feeling a sense of belonging, in choosing the kind of vocation to pursue. This opened my eyes to something I'd been missing – that the vocation came not only by looking at God and asking his opinion, but also by looking at myself and the possible places I could belong.

The following day, I was driving back to Wales, giving one of my South West regional team members a lift as far as Bristol. Somewhere on the M4, just past Reading, our conversation took an unexpected turn. "I still don't know what God's asking me to do after this doctorate," I said, "but when I become a priest I shall…"

"Hang on, what did I just say?"

It had happened. The decision had made the longest journey, from the head to the heart, and had popped out, unbidden, in the middle of our conversation. But this decision required another – what kind of priesthood?

Oxford houses many of the long established religious orders: Benedictines, Jesuits, Dominicans, Franciscans and even a Carmelite or two – but I'd never got to know any of them that well. Through Youth 2000, I did know many priests who belong to the newly-reformed orders which all, in various ways, emphasise the Blessed Sacrament and Our Lady: the Franciscans of the Renewal, Franciscans of the Immaculate, Community of St John (French-based and Dominican-inspired), and the Community of the Beatitudes (Carmelite roots). I respected greatly what these orders stood for – but the Saturday talk had helped me to appreciate that I had no sense of belonging to any of these. I had no sense of being called to Community life, and no desire to sing psalms in choir several times a day.

If not religious life, then, I must apply to a diocese, to work under a particular bishop in his territory, in the expectation of spending my working life mostly in parish work. Which diocese? I'd only been in Nottingham for a year, and the student chaplaincy at Oxford hadn't given me any sense of connection with the Birmingham Archdiocese. My parents lived in Menevia, but I had become a Catholic as a sixth-former and left home for university a year later: no deep roots there. Ultimately, there was only one place I 'belonged' in terms of knowing and networking with the priests: Cardiff. This became clear by mid-January, so I made approaches to my University Chaplain in Cardiff, and soon found myself meeting monthly with Cardiff's Vocations Director.

Time sped past. By July 1999 I had submitted my PhD thesis. In September, I entered St John's Seminary at Wonersh, near Guildford in Surrey. The following month I returned to Cardiff to defend my thesis: the internal examiner, knowing I was training for the priesthood, took great delight in slowly and painfully pointing out: "Mr Leyshon, I've been checking on your references, and I've found one which is wrong!" Horror of horrors – was this going to undermine my whole thesis? I was instructed to turn to page 92, where a chapter began with the only Bible quote in the whole thesis. The examiner pointed to the text (from Genesis 15:5) and observed that it was not from Genesis 1:16, as my erroneous label proclaimed! The thesis passed, as did my embarrassment at misreading the results of a Bible search engine!

At the same time as I was submitting my thesis, Cardiff was hit by its second scandal concerning an abusive priest. During my second year at seminary Archbishop Ward was replaced temporarily by an Apostolic Administrator. Archbishop Peter Smith was appointed and installed as Cardiff's new bishop as I began my third year of studies. While these were unsettling times for myself and the other Cardiff students at Wonersh, they did not dent my sense of being called to Cardiff. The existence of one or two rotten apples did not change my sense of belonging to the good priests I had met since 1995.

Seminary contained its own challenges. I'd asked to stay on British soil rather than go to Rome, knowing that as a lifelong academic it would be important for me to take the opportunity for as many pastoral placements as possible, to build up experience – without the extra hurdle of a different language and culture. As I had expected, the main critique made of me by the seminary staff, was of a certain awkwardness in the way I related to other people. I felt that the solution lay in a 'head' approach of learning how best to relate to others in various circumstances. The seminary staff, however, hoped that I could learn to connect with my intuitive side – a 'heart' solution. With no sense that I was developing in the way the seminary staff hoped, I made a retreat in 2003, wondering whether I shouldn't join the Jesuits as a priest-astronomer, or follow an Oxford friend into the Dominicans; but nothing dented my deep sense of belonging to the Cardiff Archdiocese, and of being called to be a missionary to South Wales.

A key part of any seminarian's journey is applying for Candidacy – the Church's formal declaration that a person is suitable to be ordained priest. Early in 2004 I applied for this, but the seminary authorities made the rare step of deferring a decision rather than approving me, or giving the outright refusal which would have ended my seminary journey. I think the seminary staff were still hoping to see a natural maturing of my intuitive side.

At about the same time, there was a change of personnel in the human development (counselling) staff at the seminary. Working with a new staff member, it was agreed that I could try something more 'head-centred' (in psychological jargon, a 'cognitive-behavioural' approach). This eventually proved to be quite fruitful, but took a long time to organise. In the summer of 2005, my classmates proceeded to Ordination as deacons, but I was required to remain in seminary for an additional year. Yet at the same time, I notched up a First Class degree in Theology and was elected Dean (head student) by my peers. Finally, almost two years after applying, I was granted Candidacy at the end of 2005.

With three other seminarians, I was ordained Deacon in June 2006. I spent three months (at my own request) undertaking some additional training in culturally-relevant mission with the Sion Community in Essex, before being assigned to St Dyfrig's Parish in Pontypridd, just outside Cardiff, in October. Archbishop Peter Smith ordained me as priest in May 2007.

A moment of clarity on the banks of the Medway in 1993 has resulted in me now being pastor on the banks of the Taff in 2010. The priestly work in Pontypridd is immensely varied. The satisfaction of celebrating daily Mass and regular baptisms is spiced by the occasional joy of welcoming a returning sinner to the church (I have literally jumped for joy after the penitent's departure on two such occasions) but also, of course, tempered by the odd early-morning calls to the hospital, the necessity of preparing funerals for unknown Catholics, and the incessant ringing of the telephone (not least from drunk students in the small hours wanting to know Mass times). The variety of what is required of a general purpose pastor is exceptionally wide, and not for the faint-hearted.

Sometimes people suggest that I have "wasted" the great investment of time and money in my education at Oxford, and to doctorate level, by choosing the path of the priesthood. I beg to differ. It was my journey through Oxford and Cardiff which led to my being able to be this kind of priest, here and now. I still enjoy visiting a science conference each year and giving the occasional talk on topics in science and religion – and I don't think my heart would have achieved the deep commitment required for keeping up with journals and churning out the grant applications required of today's professional scientist. In the Church, we have a special word for when a person gives up time, talent, and investment in seeking God's will. The word is not WASTE – it is SACRIFICE.

Since my Ordination, events have proceeded at a breathtaking pace. Our local Dean, in Caerphilly, was asked by Archbishop Peter to form a "team ministry" together with the priest overseeing me in Pontypridd to cover our parishes and the vacant Rhondda parish. In jest, I suggested that the priest overseeing me should move into the Rhondda, and a local priest about to retire should move in to keep an eye on me. By October 2007, this is exactly what happened. By early 2008 I was, in effect, Parish Priest of Pontypridd, and as I write this in February 2010, I have had a curate – a priest on loan from India – for two months! Truly, the stone which the builders rejected has become a cornerstone, and only the Lord can do this! Here I am Lord: I come to do your will.

A Pilot – or a Priest?

Fr Paul Moss is Vocations Director for the Archdiocese of Birmingham and also lectures in Philosophy at Oscott College, Birmingham. He was ordained priest on 23 July 2005 and served for four years in parishes and schools in Coventry.

Oscott College is the seminary for the Archdiocese of Birmingham and lies right under the flight path of Birmingham International Airport. I recall my very first visit there, with the frequent sound of aircraft overhead. I wondered how I could possibly cope living there, if I were to be accepted as a seminarian, because for so many years all I had wanted to do was become a pilot. What if I were to regret the decision and have the continual reminder or distraction of an alternative life literally hanging over my head? As things turned out I was sent to the English College in Rome, where the noises turned out to be crowds of tourists and the drone of seagulls!

This is to jump ahead, however, for until I was seventeen, I had never considered the possibility of becoming a priest. So what happened? Throughout my secondary school years, although I did not become an atheist, my faith certainly receded into the background. I had been baptised as an infant and went to a Catholic primary school, but on going to secondary school I more or less stopped attending Mass and could see little relevance in God and the Church. Looking back it is too easy to blame poor catechesis or whatever, and sometimes I think the journey of faith includes periods of absence that in the longer view only help to strengthen a renewal of faith when the Lord finally gets us back! And get me back he did, but slowly, gently and gradually, which is usually the Lord's way.

On all journeys there tend to be certain landmarks or signs along the way that stick out, as well as quieter more uneventful stretches. It is the same in our journey of faith, our journey to Eternal Life, or even the liturgical year, which is punctuated by the great festivals of Easter and Christmas. As I was growing up, without realising it, I was searching for what would me make me happy in life and bring me true fulfilment. For many years I thought that a career in aviation would answer this yearning, and so I gave little or no thought to other possibilities. As a result of being granted a flying scholarship from the Royal Air Force when I was seventeen, I gained my private pilot's licence and was indescribably happy. Or so I thought. Quite soon after achieving my life's ambition, I began to be visited by niggles of doubt as to whether this was in fact what would bring me true happiness for the rest of my life.

More or less at the same time, I was also questioning my identity as a Catholic. Being at a non-Catholic secondary school made me aware of being Catholic even though I was unsure what it meant to me. Each Tuesday morning a couple of Catholic teachers would take the Catholic students for prayers and give a short talk on an aspect of the faith. I vividly recall the morning on which the doctrine of Apostolic Succession was mentioned; for it was the first time I had heard of such an idea. It really caught my imagination. It set off a chain of reasoning in my mind that led me to see the unique importance of the Catholic priesthood. I then wanted to explore some questions to do with my faith and was encouraged to speak to my Parish Priest. I was very nervous about approaching him since I had never really spoken to a priest before and assumed that he would tell me off for not going to Mass regularly!

Still, I summoned up the courage to make an appointment to see him and set off with some trepidation. This was to be a crucial moment in my journey of faith and vocation. I must have been speaking with my Parish Priest for well over an hour during which we had an excellent conversation touching on many things. I was struck at how normal, how ordinary he appeared. He even had a sense of humour! Towards the end of the conversation, I explained how I had gained my pilot's licence but that I was not entirely sure if I wanted to proceed with flying as a career after school and university. Then he asked me a question: "Paul, have you ever thought of being a priest?" My immediate reaction was to laugh out loud and reply "No". Looking back I can see how the Holy Spirit sowed the seed of my priestly vocation at that moment. I cannot describe it as a dramatic conversion experience but rather as a firm yet gentle nudge towards the Lord.

As the days, weeks and months followed, I became aware of a persistent niggle at the back of my mind about this idea of being a priest. It all seemed a little ridiculous as I did not even go to Mass very often; nor did I really know much about what the life of the priesthood entailed; moreover I was fairly ignorant about much of the Bible and the Church's teachings. I did talk things through with some supportive teachers at school who encouraged me to read more, and to speak again with my Parish Priest, which I did. He then urged me to start coming to Mass, to become an altar server and to get more involved in the life of the parish, which I did.

Throughout my last year at school, while I was focusing on my A-levels and applying for a place at university, there were times when the idea either drifted away, or when I wanted the idea of priesthood to disappear. Yet the niggle would always re-emerge, sometimes annoyingly so! Thoughts about giving up on the possibility of having a family, or working for some good cause to make the world a better place, seemed like real obstacles to my pursuing the idea of becoming a priest. Still, that niggle would always return.

Although at the beginning of my final year at school I had decided to go to university and study mechanical engineering, by the time my A-level results came out I was very unenthusiastic about it. I just didn't have any passion for engineering and had only applied because it seemed like a good degree for a pilot to have! But as the thoughts of the priesthood were still there I decided to reapply and study theology. This meant having an unintended gap year, during which I worked mostly at an examinations board in my home town of Oxford, but I did manage to go to the Holy Land for two weeks, during which I read the Catechism of the Catholic Church from cover to cover, learning much about my faith in the process.

The year between school and university was a very important one. It gave me a chance to get more involved in the life of my parish, and to continue to grow in my recently re-found faith. I also had the joy of getting to know my Parish Priest and we developed a life-long friendship that has been of inestimable value and support. Hospitality was certainly one of the hallmarks of the presbytery and it was often that I found myself invited for meals where there would invariably be visiting priests and religious from all over the world. I met seminarians from Rome, priests from Africa and the Americas, and monks from England. I began for the first time to appreciate the depth and breadth of the Church's life and started to wonder, probably out of mere curiosity, if I might be being called to the religious life. I had no strong desire for Community life as such, nor did any particular religious orders attract me, since I didn't really know any. So I set out to learn all about the Benedictines, the Franciscans, the Carmelites, Jesuits and Dominicans, mostly by reading books, but I also spent a few days at a Benedictine Abbey. Although I very much enjoyed my stay I did not feel any tug on my heart to join!

I also made some great new friends at work, where many young people and students were employed. I remember conversation turning one day to what we would all be doing in a few years time. I was very hesitant about admitting that I might become a priest and feared what kind of a reaction such an admission would incur. Eventually I thought I'd just dive in and boldly said, as if I were joking, that I intended to be a priest. The response was not at all what I had expected. People were interested, complimentary and very encouraging. This became one of the first steps towards discovering a real confidence in speaking about God and my faith in public, something that would have completely embarrassed me previously.

The following year I started a theology degree at Birmingham University, where I again made some enduring friendships and thoroughly enjoyed three great years of fun and a usual student lifestyle, which I won't go into here! Even though there were times when I felt the call to the priesthood wane or even disappear, the sense of vocation gently yet steadily grew. During my final year my Vocations Director, with whom I had been in contact since I was eighteen, asked me whether I wanted to apply that year. This time my response to a priest asking me about the priesthood was "Yes!".

To my surprise the Archbishop wanted me to study at the English College in Rome where, after the first few weeks of bliss and excitement, the reality of priestly formation set in. There followed six years, which were among both the happiest and most difficult of my life. This was the place where I really learned to pray and to trust in God. Looking back I am certain that the prayers of many faithful people back home sustained me through much of my time in Rome. There were moments when I wanted to leave, convinced that it was all a dreadful mistake. How could I possibly take a promise of celibacy; how could I embrace the Cross that is at the heart of following Jesus? I recall one afternoon praying in the College church when I was quite down. Looking at a statue of the Cross I was certain that I wasn't cut out for pain and sacrifice. Then the Lord must have helped me, because I suddenly received a keen insight that to embrace the sacrifices asked of a priest does not lead down a path to captivity but rather to real freedom and joy, if lived with trust in God's providence.

I remember another occasion when the Lord nudged me back on track. In my last year in Rome, I was convinced that I should definitely leave the seminary. I went for a melancholic stroll round the city and eventually found myself in a church gazing upon Caravaggio's *Call of St Matthew*. I had a very powerful experience of Jesus pointing his finger at me as if he were saying "Yes, I know all about you, I know your faults and weaknesses, and all the sins you have committed, but I still want you to be a priest."

Above all, I have learned, and am still learning, that the path of discipleship, this road of conversion and transformation, does not just take place when we are young and in seminary. It is a life-long journey in which we constantly learn about God's presence and his grace. I would say that despite having changed so much in my six years in Rome, I have changed even more in the few years since my priestly ordination. I can only pray that I will continue to be changed by the Lord, and that many more young men and women will follow the path of their vocation because, despite the challenges and difficulties that any life brings, to follow God's will is simply the most wonderful thing in the world.

No Greater Honour

Fr RICHARD NESBITT

Fr Richard Nesbitt is Vocations Director for the Archdiocese of Westminster. He was ordained priest on 16 June 2007.

For the first eighteen years of my life I knew nothing of God. It is possible in Britain today to live from the cradle to the grave without any direct contact with religious practice, simply because it is not part of the landscape of your family or community. This was my experience. I was born in Edinburgh and brought up in a loving middle-class family, which moved down to England when I was six. My parents had decided that they would allow my sister and I to choose our own religious path in life – a decision which I can understand but which in practice meant that I grew up thinking of religion as little more than a subject you studied at school. Symbolically I had given up R.E. at the age of fourteen – other subjects just seemed much more 'useful'. My life instead was focused on doing well at school, enjoying sport and music.

Then, on 23 October 1984, the day of my eighteenth birthday, my life changed forever. I was watching the evening news when I saw a report by the BBC journalist Michael Buerk about the famine in Ethiopia. It showed scenes of human suffering that I had never seen before – devastating in both the sheer number of people involved and in the harrowing depiction of the impact on individuals: mothers sitting listlessly in the baking sun with a vacant, lost look in their eyes, their starving babies mere skeletal bundles by their sides. Many did not even have the strength to brush the flies from their dust-covered faces. This refugee camp where thousands were seeking sanctuary had become in the words of the report "hell on earth".

Instantly, I began to see the world in a new way – my own personal ambitions and success seemed trivial in the face of such suffering. I felt an emotional (I would now say a spiritual) connection with those people which the life I was living seemed to offer no way of realising. So I decided to take a year off after finishing school so that I could go out there to make that connection real. 'There' turned out to be not Africa but India and six months work on a school project near Delhi.

It was in India that I experienced my own poverty – a poverty which I came to understand as a spiritual emptiness. India is the greatest religious melting pot in the world – a country in which Hinduism, Sikhism, Buddhism, Islam and Christianity all meet and, with varying degrees of peacefulness, co-exist. I lived with a Sikh family, took part in Hindu festivals, sat under the tree where the Buddha received Enlightenment and shared long train journeys with Christian missionaries. For the first time in my life I experienced religion not as an optional extra but as the heart-beat of people's everyday lives. I also learnt that there is a value to every human person which has nothing to do with the external but everything to do with the human soul. I received infinitely more than I gave during those six months and was humbled by the generosity and vivacity of the people I lived and worked with – people who on the surface were materially so much poorer than me but who had an understanding of their own identity and culture which I did not have. Those six months blew my horizons wide open.

I returned to England to study English Literature at Cambridge University. I threw myself into student life, exhilarated by all the opportunities it had to offer. Having been brought up in a fairly sheltered family environment, it felt liberating suddenly to be plunged into a world of such freedom. For someone like myself, very much searching for a spiritual and moral compass in my life, that inevitably meant losing myself down some false paths. However, looking back, these were precious days of exploration and discovery with several key friendships forged which have been a wonderful source of nourishment and support ever since.

When I graduated, I knew what I didn't want to do – the prestigious, highly individualistic City jobs which had tempted so many of my university friends. I wanted to find a job which was more than a job – something more like a way of life which would help me to help others. To pay the bills I drifted into teaching English as a foreign language and got a job at a Cambridge language school. I discovered the beauty of teaching – the privilege of helping others to express their thoughts and ideas so that they in turn become your teachers.

Then, one evening, I met a young Polish couple in a pub in Cambridge with whom I shared a love of Guinness! They told me of all the changes which were happening in their country (this was 1989 and after the fall of the Berlin Wall the Communist regimes in Eastern Europe were tumbling like dominoes) and how much native-speaker English teachers were now going to be needed in Poland. By the end of the evening I had contact addresses for schools in a Polish city I had never even heard of and a month later I found myself arriving by train in that same city (which was called Wrocław). Just as I had been greeted at Delhi airport by a young man holding a card with my name written on, so now I was welcomed by a father and son bearing a similar card. Little did I realise that night that this city and its people would change my life forever.

It was an extraordinary time to arrive in Poland. After decades of Nazi and then Communist rule the people were finally free. I arrived when they were preparing for their first Presidential elections with Lech Wałęsa's beaming face plastered over every available wall space and bus shelter. There was a thrilling mood of optimism and hope – after all those grey years of bitter oppression people believed that they could at last reach for the stars. For many learning English was a key to this, which meant that I was bombarded with requests for lessons. I began my day at the offices of a group of journalists who, now free from censorship, had set up their own newspaper to report the truth as they saw it; then I travelled to a company of architects who, after years of designing uniform shoe-box buildings for the Communist authorities, could now design buildings of vision and innovation and so enter international competitions. I taught groups of artists, actors, university students, even army officers – each group in their own way hungry for English to help them build a new life.

Then one day I was asked if I could find time for one more group – a group of Catholic priests at the city's Cathedral. I immediately agreed, not least because I had been struck by how often my other students talked about the importance of faith and the Church in their lives. I was intrigued to see for myself what this Church was all about. The priests were a great group – funny, lively, very human. When one of them invited me to visit his church the following Sunday I readily agreed.

I remember that Sunday so vividly. It was a freezing

February day and the little round church, called St Martin's, was buried in a deep snowfall. I arrived a little before 10 o'clock, walked up the steps and pulled back the heavy red curtains at the entrance which were meant to keep out the cold. Inside I found about a hundred people of all ages whispering in excited little huddles, kneeling in prayer or sitting in silence staring at a beautifully carved crucifix behind the altar. Suddenly a bell rang, everyone stood up and the priest appeared dressed in purple robes.

My 'first Mass' was difficult for me – not only was everything in a foreign language but also I felt oppressed by the gloomy atmosphere (I had no idea at the time what Lent was!). After a while I decided there was no point in staying so I crept quietly to the door. But when I reached the thick red curtains and pulled them apart, I looked out and saw a scene which stopped me in my tracks. The street outside was totally lifeless – the bare branches of the trees, the total greyness of the landscape, nothing moving. I suddenly realised that this was a picture of my life – for all my travels and experiences there was an aching emptiness within me. I had no idea where I wanted to go and yet I felt I could not stay in the church either. I had been moved by a power which seemed to unite the people inside but I had also felt excluded. I stepped outside but at the same time felt drawn to stay so I spent the next half-hour walking in circles around the church. After the Mass, 'my priest' came out to find me and taking one look at the trail of footprints around his church, he smiled, gave me a hug and told me not to worry but to come back the next week if I wanted.

A week later I woke up early and without thinking too much about it, caught the tram to St Martin's. My second Mass was a completely different experience – I still understood very little but I was moved by the rhythmic melody of the language, by the deep prayerfulness of the congregation and by the beautiful crucifix. I stayed to the end of the Mass and when the priest came to find me, this time I hugged him and asked if he would have time to meet me and answer some questions I had. He smiled and immediately agreed. After twenty-five years God had finally caught my attention!

How to explain the journey that followed... Almost overnight everything changed – the books I wanted to read, how I chose to spend my free time, the things I wanted to talk about. I met with the priest after our English lessons and would bombard him with questions about the most fundamental aspects of the faith – about why Jesus had to die, the role of Mary, who the Holy Spirit was as well as about the Church's moral teaching. What was extraordinary was that we had almost no common language – just a little bit of French and German half-remembered from school, some extremely basic Polish and English (he specialised in Beatles' song titles!) and diagrams if words ran out – and yet we managed to understand each other perfectly. I was completely amazed by the way he was able to answer all my questions by referring everything I threw at him to the foundation of faith which his life was built upon. Never before in my life had I met someone who understood so well exactly who he was and what he was living for. Here, I instinctively felt, was the truth that I had been looking for all these years.

During the months that followed I began to discover God. I spent long hours in churches just sitting on my own in silence, yet realising that I was not on my own –

that the One who had created me was watching over me with eyes of love. I began to enter into a relationship with God through prayer and through reading His Word. I devoured the Scriptures, amazed that on those pages I was reading my own story – the Prodigal son, the man born blind, the woman at the well, Zacchaeus… I was impressed too by how the congregation at St Martin's lived out their faith in their everyday lives with projects for the homeless and housebound and with their constant support for each other. I was also blessed to travel with a group from the parish on pilgrimage to Rome where we were granted a private audience with Pope John Paul II – a man whose personal example and teaching was to have a profound effect on me in the years to come. In all of this I came to understand that all the deepest undercurrents of my life – the search for truth, an impatience with compromise, a desire for commitment, to work for the common good, a hunger to make the world more human, to live out a deep solidarity with others – all of these found their fulfilment in God. I realised that in all my explorations it had been Jesus I was truly seeking and in looking back on my life I could see his features becoming clearer and clearer through all I had experienced.

There were mountains to climb – not least the pain I knew all this would cause to my parents – but at last I asked to be received into the Church. This took place at St Martin's at the Easter Vigil in 1994. When everyone had lit their candles from the paschal candle and the little church was ablaze with light, I stepped forward, dressed in a long white robe and accompanied by my godparents, to receive the gift of new life through baptism. The church resounded with a song of "Alleluia", so long-awaited through all of Lent and through all my life. Later, I came up to the altar to be nourished for the first time by the Body and Blood of Christ.

The greatest surprise of that extraordinary night was the voice I heard within me calling me to become a priest. It seemed incredible and all I could think of was my own unworthiness but there it was all the same. After my baptism I set up a Catholic language school with a Polish friend in a parish in Wrocław. We wanted to teach the 'whole person' – preparing the students for all the standard English exams but also creating a community in which they could also talk about their spiritual selves, their hopes and values. For the next six years this great venture was at the heart of my life with over two hundred students enrolled every year – children and adults, with weekend trips to the Polish mountains and summer camps by the Baltic.

During all this time, the voice calling me to the priesthood grew and grew. I moved into the presbytery of the parish where our school was located and became part of the parish team. I also became the parish gardener – a great way I discovered to get to know parishioners who would stop and talk as I was planting a new shrub. My Polish was by now pretty fluent and so I began to be asked to speak to school groups and youth clubs about my conversion experience. I realised that all we receive from God we are to share with others. Nothing gave me greater joy. I discovered the grace of an annual eight-day retreat following the Ignatian Spiritual Exercises at a monastery in Kraków. My love of Scripture grew and grew – those words of the two disciples on the road to Emmaus: "did not our hearts burn within us while he was talking to us on the road" (Lk 24-32) encapsulated everything I felt when I was near to God. Perhaps the greatest sign that I received was the grace to begin to believe that I would be able to live a celibate life. When I first came to Poland I had wanted to get married – to be a husband and a father. Yet with time, almost without my being aware of it, this desire began to fade just as my desire to live for God intensified. I began to see celibacy not as a burden but as a gift, bringing the freedom to be totally available for God and for others.

Perhaps the greatest question for me became not "Is God calling me to become a priest?" but "Where is he calling me to be a priest?" Every summer I used to return to England for a month or so, travelling by coach to Victoria station in London. One summer I discovered Westminster Cathedral just around the corner from the station – a building I fell in love with from the very first moment I entered its sublime interior. It is a house of God, pulsing with his presence. Although I had never imagined myself living in London, God made it increasingly clear to me that this was where he was calling me to be. So at the end of the Jubilee Year of 2000, I sent off my application to be considered for formation to the priesthood for the diocese of Westminster. Just as God had sent guides to help me on my way in Poland so he continued to lead me through the kindness and care of wonderful guides in London and, by the grace of God, I was accepted for formation.

Leaving Poland, leaving the school and all my friends, was heartbreaking but joyful as well as we rejoiced in the miracle of God's mercy and providence – that the lost sheep who had arrived in Poland more than ten years earlier was now returning home to become a shepherd for others. I arrived at Allen Hall seminary in Chelsea on 10 September 2001 with my backpack and guitar. The following morning I woke up to begin my new life in this haven of peace and quiet, just as the world was waking up to the terrible pictures of the 11 September terrorist attacks on the Twin Towers in New York. Those pictures, played over and over again, made so clear, just like those images from the Ethiopian famine back in 1984, how much the world needed a new heart and a renewed desire for reconciliation and true justice. A priest is one who is called to be a prophet, a builder of this new order, and so it felt like an extraordinary calling to mission to begin this new chapter of my life on that day of all days.

The six years of formation which followed were amongst the happiest of my whole life. After all the busyness of running a school for six years, what a gift it was to have the time and space to study again, and to deepen my relationship with God through a daily life centred on prayer and the Eucharist. A seminary is a place where that delicate shoot of God's calling can be nurtured and nourished. As time goes on that tender plant needs to be prepared for life beyond the protective glass and so the seminarian is increasingly sent out into the world to parishes, hospitals, prisons and schools. He grows from a disciple (a 'learner') to an apostle ('one who is sent'), whilst always, of course, remaining a learner. It is humbling to reflect on the number of people whose wisdom and guidance contribute to the shaping of a priest's heart. This was my thought as I looked out at all the people who had gathered on Saturday 16 June 2007 for my Ordination at Westminster Cathedral – friends from university, from Poland and from the parishes and communities in which I had served in during my seminary days. The greatest gift of all was to see my parents sitting in the front pew, reconciled through God's grace to their son's calling.

I give thanks to God every day for my life as a priest. I love the extraordinary ways in which God walks beside us in the apparent ordinariness of everyday parish life – the ways in which he invites us to come to know him better and to be as Christ to each other through our highs and lows. The grace of Confession, the gift of the Eucharist and his Word freely offered to us with unconditional love – words cannot express the beauty of it all. Added to all this has been the honour of being asked to take on the role of Vocations Director for the Archdiocese of Westminster. It feels like my journey has come full circle – just as I have been encouraged and guided by so many wise souls, so now I am called to serve as a guide and companion for others on their journey of exploring God's will for their lives. I can imagine no greater honour.

From Particles to Priesthood

Fr ANDREW PINSENT

Formerly a particle physicist at CERN, Fr Pinsent is now a priest of the Diocese of Arundel and Brighton and Research Director of the Ian Ramsey Centre for Science and Religion at the University of Oxford. He was ordained on 3 September 2005.

Twenty years ago, I was monitoring the tracks of particle collisions in a vast underground laboratory in Switzerland. Today, the whole aim of my life is to serve God in the priesthood, to provide whatever people need in order to be happy forever in heaven. I do not claim to have chosen to become a priest, since such vocations come from God. I am grateful, however, to God for giving me the grace to answer the call. As you may be wrestling with a similar decision, to accept or reject a call to the priesthood or some other vocation, I hope that this story may be some encouragement to you.

Rather than planning to become a priest, the earliest aspiration that I can recall was to become an astronaut. This desire to journey to strange new worlds was accompanied by an enthusiasm for all kinds of science and technology. As my knowledge became more informed, I began to concentrate on physics, which I recognised increasingly to be the basis of all the particular sciences in which I was interested. At the age of fourteen, my father took me to visit the colleges of Oxford. I was awed by the atmosphere of learning and the beautiful medieval architecture, which I recognise today to be a sign of the Catholic origins of this great university. At the age of seventeen, thanks to hard work and dedicated teachers, I was offered a place to read Physics at Merton College and later received a scholarship. After three happy years, I was awarded a First Class Honours degree before reaching the age of twenty-one.

Since I wanted to extend my study of physics further, I applied to read for a doctorate and was offered a place in a team at Oxford finishing part of an experiment called DELPHI. The timing of this offer was providential since DELPHI was approaching completion in preparation for the start of the Large Electron Positron collider (LEP) at the CERN laboratory in Switzerland. The LEP was a ring-shaped machine, over five miles in diameter, designed to collide beams of matter and antimatter to simulate the conditions of the Big Bang, a theory of the early universe first proposed, incidentally, by a largely forgotten Catholic priest, Mgr Georges Lemaître. During this period of preparation, Tim Berners-Lee, a British physicist also working at CERN, designed the 'world-wide web' (www), establishing the basis of the modern Internet. Working on the DELPHI project, I spent two years testing equipment and writing software for the start of operation and had written, by the age of twenty-four, one of the first doctorates based on data from the new collider.

At this point in my life, however, I experienced a sense of dissatisfaction. I could not continue to study physics without starting to turn research into my career, but I was unsure that I wanted to commit my whole life to physics. From the age of twelve, I had been blessed by a complete confidence in the Catholic Faith, thanks I believe to the prayers and example of my parents as well as my grandmother's daily Rosary. I had also managed to continue attending Mass even when living at the CERN laboratory seven days a week. Yet I not only wanted to fulfil my Catholic obligations, but to find some way of sharing this unique, wonderful faith with others. What, then, was I meant to do with my life?

In retrospect, God had already shown me the answer. At the age of nineteen, I had received a sudden, completely unexpected call to become a priest. Again at the age of twenty-two, when I was walking back to my apartment and thinking only of software for our experiment, I suddenly *knew* that I would become a priest. What was peculiar about both occasions was that this call seemed to come from nowhere, at least not from any previous train of thought in my own mind. While difficult to put into words, the experience was rather like having a door open into my mind and being able suddenly to see a different life beyond the door. Nevertheless, I tried subsequently to forget about these experiences. While I had a great respect for the priests that I knew, and was grateful for their sacrifices, nothing about the priestly way of life seemed remotely appealing to me. I did not know anyone training to be a priest and priesthood also meant celibacy, whereas my plan for my own life was to get married.

I persisted therefore in trying to build my home in this world. At twenty-four I switched from research to business, working first for a scientific consultancy firm and then starting my own company. This work, which took me to the United States and Latin America, was creative and rewarding. In my late twenties, I was sometimes commuting across the Tropic of Capricorn each morning, driving north out of the great city of São Paulo to work for one of the new computer and electronics companies in this rapidly developing region.

Throughout my twenties, I also had several girlfriends, yet I became mystified over the way in which none of these relationships seemed to last, as if God was intervening on each occasion to prevent me settling down. I also became conscious of the many problems of the Church, including an ageing priesthood. At one time, I heard a homily in which a Verona Father asked directly, "Who will take my place?" Yet while I fervently hoped that others would come forward, I was not keen on sacrificing myself.

Finally, however, at the age of thirty-one, the call to the priesthood returned in a new and urgent form. Whereas on previous occasions I had received the intuition that I would or should become a priest, this time the call was insistent that I should respond at once. The sensation was almost like being pulled away physically from my previous way of life. The turning point was over a cup of coffee shared with my sister, Jane. When I told her, "I think I may have a vocation," she said to me, "That's great news, Andrew! What have you got to lose? We'll all be dead in forty years!" With that response, the futility of trying to build a permanent home in this world became obvious. This world provides the means to true happiness, since it is in this life that God offers us the opportunity to know and love him and the freedom to accept or deny this friendship. Nevertheless, except for human souls and the angels, nothing in this world, including the cosmos as a whole, lasts forever. Since we are all going to lose our lives in this world, I realised that I had no reason not to sacrifice everything else for the sake of union with God. Besides, I would only be exchanging what would soon be lost anyway for the chance to bring eternal life to others and hopefully myself. Even from a business perspective, I could therefore obtain no better return on the investment of my life. Finally, therefore, I surrendered to God's call. I applied to my home diocese of Arundel and Brighton and Bishop Cormac sent me to start training at the Venerable English College in Rome in October 1998.

The next few years were daunting in certain ways, since I had to start again with a new way of life, in a new country and with a new language. Yet although I had many challenges, I never experienced the slightest doubt about my vocation, even on those occasions when I wanted to have doubts. What helped to sustain me were two principles explained by the rector of the seminary, Mgr Adrian Toffolo, when I first arrived. First, he said to the new seminarians that we would be happy to the extent that we prayed, highlighting that the source of our strength to be fruitful could only come from God. Indeed, the rector reinforced this lesson himself by praying for hours every morning. Second, he cited a quotation from *Pastores Dabo Vobis* in which the Holy Father urged seminarians to study for the sake of the salvation of their brothers and sisters (paragraph 51). In other words, we were not to regard academic training as simply a hurdle to be overcome, but a vital aspect of our training that could help bring people to salvation.

On this basis, I worked hard to absorb every scrap of knowledge or insight that the courses offered, as my earlier training in physics and technology was gradually complemented by philosophy and theology. Nevertheless, I also developed a great love of many of the subjects we studied for their own sake, especially philosophy. Training in Rome brought several further benefits, including the advantage of studying in a thoroughly Catholic culture blessed by many visible fruits of the faith. As a consequence, when I started with a friend to write a catechetical course at the seminary, published later by the Catholic Truth Society as the *Evangelium* course, we used images of great religious art that we had experienced in Italy.

Following Ordination on 3 September 2005 my life has taken ever more unplanned and unexpected directions. First, my love of philosophy was given further scope by the award of a graduate position in the United States completing a PhD with Prof. Eleonore Stump, a famous analytical philosopher, teacher, and expert on Aquinas. I therefore spent four years dividing my time between a parish and a university, and between England and the United States. With this PhD completed, I was offered a position at Oxford in the theology faculty. I now divide my time between Oxford, where I am Research Director of the Ian Ramsey Centre for Science and Religion, and Epsom, where I assist the parish priest. Besides my formal duties, I am working on a range of catechetical projects, seeking ever more ways to communicate the gospel. Apart from the *Evangelium* course, I have also helped to write the *Credo* pocket catechism and the *Apologia* book of apologetics in recent years, and am now working on a Confirmation course. While my life so far as a priest might seem unusual, in truth there is no such thing as a standard pattern. God seems to like variety in the vocations of his diocesan priests, and while all are called by Christ to follow him, the precise path each one takes is a unique story.

This personal story confirms some basic truths about vocations today. First, it is easy to be deceived by technological and cultural changes into assuming that a religious calling belongs to an out-of-date world. Yet God is still calling men to the priesthood today, even in the world of the Internet and particle accelerators. Indeed, such callings are to be expected, given that the demands of human salvation as well as the desire to find a life of genuine fulfilment are as imperative today as they have always been. Second, one does not have to like in advance what one is called to do, but one does need to be able to pray, "Thy will be done." In other words, it is sufficient to ask God for the will to respond, if the call is genuine, for it is God who makes a positive response possible. Third, the priesthood is supernaturally fruitful. My experience of priesthood has been one of unending fruitfulness and I am never bored and never lonely. Every day I offer the Body and Blood of Christ to our Heavenly Father. Every day I may receive some new insight, or have some conversation that may change a person's life. Every day I may be working with friends to develop new means to pass on the gospel to others. Every day I may even free a soul from mortal sin in Confession, re-storing the gift of grace and the hope of heaven, which is infinitely greater than anything this world has to offer.

I would like to conclude with some parts of the prayer for vocations addressed to Our Lady at the end of *Pastores Dabo Vobis*:

O Mother of Faith, you accompanied to the Temple the Son of Man, the fulfilment of the promises given to the fathers; give to the Father for his glory the priests of your Son, protect their growth, in their ministry accompany your sons, O Mother of Priests. Amen.

Leaving Fingerprints

Fr STEVEN PURNELL

Fr Steven Purnell is priest in charge of the Church of Our Lady and St Peter, East Grinstead. He was ordained priest for the Diocese of Arundel and Brighton in 1996.

L eaving fingerprints and searching for the truth – that seems to have been the story of my life so far. However, the fingerprints left behind are not mine but God's, and it is the truth of that discovery that has been my search.

Often we hear people speaking of their search for God. Sometimes, if they are of a liberal persuasion, they speak of the actual search being the important thing rather than the finding. My story is of how I found God: how I came to believe that Jesus of Nazareth was Jesus the Christ, the scandal of the particular – that in a particular place at a particular time God became man for all people in all places and times and left his fingerprints behind.

My forensic search for those fingerprints, or signs of God's presence among us, is a search for truth. "What is truth?" asked Pontius Pilate. The real question is, where is truth and who is Truth?

I was brought up in the industrial north-east of England, home of steel, shipbuilding and mining. Father had been a miner and died in his twenties. Mother was a widow with children. To say we were poor is true; to say we were working class was not the whole story. The background was mixed. One part of the family produced a few criminals and ladies of the night – not so much working class as underclass. The other half, those I had most contact with, were respectable and highly motivated, politicised folk – miners and shipyard workers – in the days when Britain really had a Communist Party worth speaking about. Many of my family were stalwarts of the Party and passionate about issues of political reform and social-economic justice.

If we had lived elsewhere it might have been different, but in the north-east Labour was the old established party of local government with its fingers in many pies and involved in many corruption scandals. So up there, to be a real political animal, a rebel, a revolutionary seeking a better world, fighting for justice against injustice and for the truth against complacency and corruption, you had to be either a Tory or a Communist. I was brought up on stories of Spain and the International Brigade during its Civil War, the Soviet Union, the Jarrow marches, the Irish Question, Poor Laws and Workhouses. The dream was of establishing a truly Communist state, a workers' paradise; of international workers' solidarity which would take us from "*each according to their ability*" to "*each according to their need*". We believed that despite China, Cuba and Russia it had not yet happened – these were states with State Capitalism and real *Communism* was only in its most infant stages. "When the Revolution comes!" was our cry.

At school I got by. Not particularly scholarly or academic I managed, in the days before continuous assessment, to cram for and pass exams. But I was political. These were the days of anti-Vietnam war marches in London and we travelled down to them. Mao and his Little Red Book were in the news. I set up a Maoist group at school, getting the books from the

Chinese Embassy, and in our little cell we discussed and memorised passages. We wore political badges and were a constant annoyance to some of our teachers. "Why? Why? Why?" we asked our teachers about the big events of the day, and through the medium of any literary or historical studies. Some may have thought we were just attempting to encourage red herrings and get off the topics on the curriculum, but our questions were genuine and revealed the youthful political fires burning within us.

I remember a history lesson about the Roman Wall – a feature close to where we lived. When the teacher mentioned 'Hadrian's Wall' I launched a tirade worthy of a Glasgow convenor calling a strike at the Clyde shipyards. "Why Hadrian's? Did he build it with his hands? Did he not have help? What about those poor foreign soldiers who built the wall? Why are they not mentioned? Isn't it typical that the ruling class has to appropriate all achievements for their own glory? Hadrian's Wall – indeed!" This at fourteen!

To the surprise of most of my teachers and all of my family, I did reasonably well at O-levels and so was persuaded not to leave school at sixteen for a life on the trawlers. It was the sea that attracted me, not the mines. So I did my A-levels, and they were a success and fitted in with my questioning of everything and the search for truth from a left-wing political perspective. However, it may seem strange to some that I did not go off to read Politics at university but chose Archaeology instead. The reason for this was the closeness of the Wall, which I had excavated with students from Durham and Newcastle Universities since my early teens. Also, of course, academic archaeology was open to a Marxist interpretation – and I was certainly far from the first to do so.

At university, politics continued to attract me more than the drugs others were doing at the time. Vietnam's war was coming to an end; the IRA were active both here on the mainland and in Northern Ireland; miners were striking and the three-day week was on. So I campaigned, protested and helped to raise money for all the favourite causes of the Left.

God had not yet appeared in my life though I believe his fingerprints were there in some of the issues of justice and peace that attracted me. But the only Christians I ever met with at university were Christian Union types. They did not seem to be interested in the things that I was into – politics, drink, women and fun. They seemed earnest, negative and committed to a form of intellectual suicide by literalist ideas concerning the Bible.

So, not thinking much about the future, other than promoting the revolution and being active and ready for it when it came, but needing money, I drifted into teaching. Ironically, I ended up teaching at a boys' public school and being the junior or assistant master to a boarding house. Because the boys would be at home for Easter, it was the practice of the school at that time to have a pre-emptive Holy Week, and invite a guest preacher to come to the school to speak at the assemblies in chapel every morning and to visit the boarding houses in the evening, holding discussion groups with the boys after they had done their prep.

One year the guest preacher was an elderly Anglican Franciscan Friar. Being present only to keep an eye on the boys I began to listen to the old man. I was amazed. Here was someone trying to live out a revolution (the kingdom of God) now and not just talking about "when the revolution comes". They say "Christianity is caught not taught". It certainly seemed to be that way with me. I started to read all I could about the Christian faith and began to meet Christians who shared the same social concerns as me. I quickly learnt that not all believed the sentiments behind the Anglican hymn:

The rich man in his castle,
The poor man at his gate,
He made them high and lowly,
He ordered their estate.

Instead I found views in the Early Church like this one of St John Chrysostom:

God in the beginning made not one man rich and another poor. Nor did he afterwards take and show to one treasures of gold, and to the other the right for searching for it. Rather he left the earth free to all alike.

The more I studied the more I became convinced that my politics were in fact motivated by ethics and not Marxism; that the International Brotherhood of the Proletariat was often far from international and generally very selective; that cultural issues were more important than economic and political ones; and, to quote G.K. Chesterton (whom I started to read),

If the problem of happiness were solved by economic comfort, the classes who are more comfortable would be the most happy, which is absurd.

The desire for peace and justice in the world, truth and happiness, the dignity of the human person – these were the fingerprints of God on my world. God's biggest fingerprint on the world was Jesus – God touching the human condition, being part of it. God becoming man in a particular place and time so that we might become close to God. The real revolution, I began to believe, was the rule of God, the kingdom of God, that can run through any and every human heart and cannot be identified with any one class, race, group or party. It is found in the daily choices of deciding to walk in God's way or on our own. While I sought to deepen my understanding of this and to share it with others, I discovered that God, amazingly, was now calling me to the ministry of priest and not party activist.

Consequently, I offered myself to the nearest church, the Church of England, for the training for and exercising of a priestly ministry. In the following years as an Anglican priest I continued to look for the fingerprints of God in the world and in the church. Increasingly I came to see that the Church of England had many fine Christian folk in it but it was not a church with a common mind to teach on spiritual matters or answer the pressing questions of the day. Everything seemed to be left to the opinions and feelings of individuals. Whoever could shout the loudest, press the hardest… Everyone was his or her own Pope.

Again, it was through contact with Catholics who were concerned with the same issues that I was, that I was made to consider the rather large claims of the Catholic Church to be the Church of Christ. The more I studied and looked at what it taught, the more I looked at history, the more I could see the fingerprints of God on the Church. Here was a Church not created out of politics and human sin but one founded by Christ himself to lead the people of God and be a continuation of Christ's Incarnation in the world. It was to be an instrument, herald and agent of God's rule – the Kingdom. In the High Church Anglican circles in which I mixed, it became clear to me that what was truly Catholic was not a certain style of liturgy nor particular Catholic teaching but simply being in communion with the Catholic Church, with Peter and his successors. With that link, then all the liturgy and teaching fitted in and made sense. So I became a Catholic and eventually a Catholic priest.

The passion of God's kingdom – a kingdom so immense and wonderful that it cannot be defined or limited by human politics and economics or class – still has a big place in my heart. The supreme act of the kingdom is Christ's sacrifice – the gift of himself – and that is re-presented at every Mass. I now see sacrifice, the gift of self, love, at the heart of faith and life. God's love for me and for all of us in Christ. The injustices that disturbed me as a child trouble me still, but now I trace these injustices back to a lack of love – love in our society and love in our hearts; a failure to live out what we truly are – God's beloved and loving children.

Not in My Wildest Dreams

Fr TOM SMITH

Fr Tom Smith is the Assistant Priest in the parish of St Gregory the Great, Cheltenham. He was ordained priest for the Diocese of Clifton on 5 July 2005.

The call to priesthood was so obvious, yet part of me couldn't see it. I was half way through the second year of my History of Art degree at Manchester University and I had a decision to make, about my future, over the next twelve months. I was in love with God, eager to work in the Church, but I didn't really want to accept what I dreaded, that God might be calling me to be a priest. I dreaded it because I saw it as something irrevocable, that would determine my future without me being in control of it and, at the age of twenty, I didn't want a determined future. I dreaded it because I was acutely aware of my weaknesses – how were they going to make me suitable to serve the Eternal and Almighty God? And of course I didn't want to be presumptuous, because being a priest is something very special, not to be taken lightly, and I didn't want to appear over-confident or too eager about it. That was my situation: I had to make a decision about my future, I was aware deep down that God might be calling me to be a priest, and yet I had serious reservations about what this would entail. The clock was ticking.

The call to priesthood was obvious to others around me – one friend in particular used to call me "Fr Tom" for a bit of a lighthearted joke and I hated it. Yet, deep down I knew. One evening I was locking the church where I used to serve at Mass. I was wearing the cassock I had served in, and encountered some nuns at the door as I was about to lock it. One of the nuns, a young one, very politely said "Good evening Father". I retorted with a bit of a barb "I'm not a priest", to which she said "You might be one day", and I said something like "No I won't." How bizarre that I should react so defensively to something I was aware of but which others could see also! It is a bit like a young couple who are at that stage before they are officially an item: their friends can see the attraction between them but for some reason it's not quite as clear to them, they even get defensive when their friends suggest anything. That was me: defensive, in denial and slightly afraid.

All my life I had been aware of the priesthood and religious calling. There were the many priests who had served in my home parish, in Salisbury, where I grew up. My secondary school in Southampton, St Mary's College, was run by Brothers of Christian Instruction, two of whom were Headmasters while I was there. The school also took us to Quarr Abbey, the Benedictine Monastery on the Isle of Wight, where I had made good friends with one of the monks. Also, I was good friends with the priest who ran the Church next to where my Mum did some further studies in Southampton. At university, too, I was exposed to good examples of priesthood. Despite all these vocational influences a number of things made discernment slightly confusing for me. Firstly, I had never grown up wanting to be a priest, so was this thing I felt genuine? Secondly, at fourteen my parents got divorced and this had a huge impact on my self-confidence. Thirdly, what if I wanted to get married? Wasn't accepting the priesthood going to rule that out and was that a decision I really wanted to make at twenty? I was left with some serious thinking to do over the next year.

Unlike some priests, I didn't grow up wanting to be a priest. I didn't have any particular idea of what I wanted, from a young age all the way through to the beginning of university. The things I enjoyed most at school were sport and free time, not big indicators of any future calling. As a child I remember being taken by my Gran into church to pray on the way into town, they were quite deep moments. Being in the small, darkened, empty church with the Blessed Sacrament is something I remember as a poignant moment. I also remember, as a child, on one occasion having an indefinable feeling when seeing the priest say Mass. It was something very deep within, maybe a vocational grace God planted in me to be discovered later on. The idea of a vocation wasn't talked about at home, not on purpose, it just wasn't. My family were not overly religious, I was taken to Mass each Sunday and after my First Holy Communion I began to serve on the altar, which I loved. The faith was there but I wasn't thinking "I want to be a priest".

That early faith was to take a serious knocking when I was fourteen and my parents got divorced. That broke my heart, my world was shattered. The thing I loved most, my family, was ended. With a broken heart came anger, resentment and an independence that turned me away from my parents and a trust in formal faith but not necessarily God. I always remained an altar server, mainly out of respect for my Grandparents, but inside I didn't put much trust in the Church which as a teenager I saw as out of touch and at times very uninspiring. My main group of friends as a teenager were not Catholic and some of the people I used to hang around with had New Age leanings and a tendency to use drugs. I remember encountering a real spiritual and emotional blackness at about the age of sixteen. I didn't know who I was, I felt empty inside, and I remember crying out to God, that if he was there could he show me and help me. That moment has become part of my testimony of God's goodness to me because he answered that cry in ways beyond my wildest imagining. I had no idea as an angst-ridden, depressed teenager that God, in his time, would work so powerfully in my life.

Mixed in with all the confusion was a deeply religious sentiment because I knew that if I didn't find God, so to speak, there was little point to life. He was the only thing that could banish the darkness and therefore give my life any meaning and peace. As my relationship with God grew so did my relationship with the Catholic Church. At the age of fourteen/fifteen I had rejected the Church intellectually, but at the age of seventeen/ eighteen, after a period of rigorous questioning, I decided to accept the Catholic Church's claims to truth and God's claims in the Gospels: that He was The Way, The Truth and The Life. I had to believe something and having looked a little bit towards the religions of the east I could find nothing of substance which satiated my desire, so I decided to give the Catholic Church a go. I was convinced that that was where The Truth lay. But despite all this, the fact of the divorce had dented my confidence as a person and I couldn't stand tall and proud because I didn't feel there was much to be proud about. But my new-found interest in the Catholic faith and its importance for my emotional and spiritual survival meant that when I went off to university I started going to Mass daily.

My first year at university was all about a deep religious faith. I also got into a relationship with someone whom I ended up loving very much, but initially our relationship didn't correspond to the faith I professed – I didn't really care though. At the end of my first year that relationship broke down and we parted company on pretty cold terms, she going back to her country and me going on an E.R.A.S.M.U.S exchange to Holland of all places. Unknown to me at the time, it was going to be the wilderness where God captured my heart.

The love affair that was to engulf my life got underway a few weeks into my time in Holland. I was in the town of Leiden and had started going to St Louis' parish church. Two girls, Eliza and Gemma, approached me after Mass one day to find out who I was and to see if I wanted to go a prayer group. As I didn't really know anyone in Leiden I was very eager to go. It just so happened that Eliza and Gemma had been to the World Youth Day in Paris. Eliza had been changed by the experience and was on fire with zeal and love for God. Gemma was involved with the Charismatic Emmanuel Community. As a follow up to the Paris WYD the Emmanuel Community organised a weekend pilgrimage to the shrine of Our Lady in Beauraing in Belgium. I was told there would be prayer and we would have the relics of St Thérèse of Lisieux with us, which meant very little to me then.

That was the weekend that changed my life. God spoke to my heart, through the words of a priest, and I have never been the same since. During one of the talks the Rector of the Shrine of the Sacred Heart at Paray-le-monial, near Lyon in France, spoke to us of God's love. He was speaking in French and I had a Dutch guy kindly translating from French to English for me. It was just one sentence spoken by the priest which he repeated three times that blew me away: "Jesus loves you, Jesus loves you, Jesus loves you!" I guess I had heard these words numerous times at church over the years but somehow God had prepared my heart to really hear them this time. It finally hit home, for the first time, that God loved me! That was why I had been struggling with the faith for all those years, why I had gone to church as a little boy, why I had made the intellectual decision those few years earlier to seek God in the Catholic Church, why I tried with great difficulty to live the church's moral teaching – because GOD LOVED ME! A deep Joy engulfed my heart and I was singing all the way home on the train much to my friend Gemma's embarrassment. The last two months in Leiden shot by and it was time to make a sad farewell.

I returned to England with a renewed faith, a contagious joy and a new-found love of the God who loved me: I was eager to get involved with the Church. I decided I wanted to work with young people so I was pointed in the direction of the chaplain of the University of Salford, Fr Ian Kelly. I went to see him about working with young people and after listening to me for a while he spoke to me about the call to holiness and the life of the saints. I said to him, "I have never heard any of this before", and he told me to come back the following week. I never really did any work with young people but I went for Spiritual Direction/Counselling with Fr Ian for about a year and a half and I also got involved in the vibrant Salford Chaplaincy. One December morning in my final year I saw Fr Ian and said that I would like to take a year out for discernment, to give me time to think and pray about the future, about what

God wanted from me. I was in love with God, eager to work in the Church, but I didn't really want to accept what I dreaded, that God might be calling me to be a priest. He asked me what I wanted to discern. I said "You know I just want to go away and discern". "Discern what?", he repeated. "You know", I said, "I just want to see what God wants." "What do you want to be?", he forcefully repeated. "I want to be a priest", I said; it came out in a small voice. I felt a JCB had churned up my innards. Fr Ian went on to say that because I knew what I wanted there was no need to go away. I was shocked, the truth was finally out: what I had felt, and what those around me had seen for almost twelve months was out. I had admitted the truth I had wanted to avoid, I felt called to be a priest.

My desire to control God's call was over, the truth was out, there would be no year of procrastination for me and I would now have to end by letter a long distance relationship with someone I loved. The relationship from my first year had undergone a lot of healing during the rest of my time at university but I realised that however much I loved someone else I loved God more. I could no longer hide from that. If I loved God and wanted to follow his call it would change my life and I wouldn't be in control: that I didn't like.

I still don't like that very much. Like many people I find the main task of Christian discipleship, abandoning my life to God, quite a challenge. As a priest there are many times when you are not in control, mainly of your diary. But the amazing thing about not being in control is that God's plans are so much better than ours; he sees the bigger picture, he wants even more for you than you want yourself. He took me from being an angst-ridden, under-confident teenager to being his priest. That blows my mind away. A vocation to the priesthood never stops: we have not made it when we get to seminary, we have not made it when we are ordained, a priestly vocation is a gift to be preserved and nourished each day. It involves the struggle of allowing God to conform us to his Son, Jesus Christ the High Priest. As for any other Christian, each day is about growing as a beloved child of Our heavenly Father. We have never made it, so-to-speak, because we can never be Christ-like enough.

Being a priest has so far been a profound joy; of course there are ups and downs. One of the biggest obstacles I have had to overcome is my own feeling of inadequacy. But it is becoming slowly more apparent to me that God is not worried by my weaknesses or imperfections and if I allow these to get me down I am ceasing to be little before him, ceasing to be reliant on his power working through my life. God has blessed me tremendously as a priest and one of my highlights is working with young people. A trip to Rome that we went on a few years ago with some young people from our parish in Cheltenham stands out in my mind. The International Priest's Retreat that I went on recently in Ars was another moving and powerful experience. I came back from Ars wanting to be a priest more that I did before I was ordained!

An Effective Witness

Fr AARON SPINELLI

Fr Aaron Spinelli is part of the Guildford Parishes team ministry, where he shares pastoral responsibility for the town's three parishes. He lists amongst his responsibilities his roles as Chaplain to the Royal Surrey hospital, Chaplain to two primary schools and a secondary school. He is also a Vocations Promoter for the Diocese of Arundel and Brighton and a member of the Jesus Caritas Priestly Fraternity. He was ordained priest in August 2008.

I was ordained a priest on a rare beautiful summer's day in August 2008 in Eastbourne, East Sussex. As I look back at the photos, which take me right back to that day, when I lay before the Lord submitting the rest of my life for his work, I notice particular faces in the congregation and on the Sanctuary, faces of people that throughout my thirty years on earth have been influential in my vocation to the priesthood.

Naturally a vocation to the priesthood is a calling, an initiative from God to a man to offer his life in configuration to Christ the High Priest, servant and victim, to serve God's people. "Many are called but few are chosen" (Mt 22:14), said our Blessed Lord, so it is important to remember that God never stops calling men to serve him. However it is how one responds, whether positively or negatively, that matters. Furthermore it is how that calling is discerned, sustained and nourished by the potential priest and indeed by those around him on his journey of discernment, such as parents, friends, parish priests, seminary staff and the bishop that is of utmost importance.

It is in this non-exhaustive list that I see in each of my Ordination photos people who have helped me, encouraged me and tested me as to whether I had a genuine call from Jesus Christ. In the first place, I would put my parents. My parents come from two of the most Catholic countries in the world: Italy and the Philippines. With a heritage such as this I could not escape Catholicism! I was baptised as a baby, and made my First Holy Communion at seven. I didn't go to church all the time but I was fortunate to have attended very good Catholic schools which sustained my faith. I was asked to become an altar server when I was nine, and did so for many years. Looking back I can say that serving on the altar was a major early influence in my vocation. Altar serving for me was a privilege and I was blessed to have had a beautiful parish church with a very dignified liturgy, which gave me at an early age a sense of the mystery of God as experienced through the beautiful liturgies we celebrated. As a server I become close to the priests and in particular to the Master of ceremonies, who was a good, holy man who treated us like adults, as we were given responsibility and treated with respect. I used to look forward to serving, which I would often do twice on a Sunday!

At the age of fourteen I was confirmed by the bishop, and whilst at the time I felt nothing extraordinary had occurred, it was after that event that I began to seriously think about what I wanted to do in life. At the time the gift of Holy Spirit had endowed me with the wisdom and courage to want to become a pilot! Travelling to exotic destinations, money – literally, it was the High Life that I wanted and could see myself living. However in my heart, something began to take hold, something quite seductive: it was the priesthood. Yet in my mind, I dismissed the idea, I wanted to fly Boeing 747's.

In year 10, as it is the case today, pupils must undergo a week's work placement. I was told by my Careers Advisor that to shadow a pilot or even work at an airport was an impossibility. I was disappointed, but she asked me what else I was interested in. I said to her, "Well, the priesthood." She was quite surprised but said she would be able to fix me up with a placement. So I spent a week shadowing priests. For me, I was used to the public liturgical work of the priest but in that week I was shown what a priest did during the week. I was bowled over with admiration for what the priests did: the visiting of the sick and the lonely, the comforting of the bereaved. I noticed the priests did everything with such love, dedication and humour. That week left a deep impression on me. Over some time, an admiration for the priests had grown into a desire to be like them, in fact I wanted to be one of them. I wanted to be a priest. As a teenager I got to know and learn from many, many wonderful holy priests, who upon reflection saw a vocation in me. They gave me time and encouragement, love and support during many difficult periods during my teens for which I am indebted.

A vocation to the priesthood is a call responded to in faith and trust, however it is a call that demands a generous response from someone living in an often difficult and challenging world. In our culture many people are indifferent to religion, often hostile to the Church and organised religion; many do not understand or care about who Jesus Christ is let alone a priest. It is from this context that one's vocation can be put to the test. It is always important to ask questions, to discern and to pray. On the one hand I would think to myself that my parents and priests supported me, but what would my friends think? Would they laugh? What would other people think? Would people think I was nuts? On the other hand, I would question my worthiness and ability, my holiness and perseverance. After all, I would have to give up a lot to become a priest. I would say that these worries lasted right up until and indeed beyond my ordination!

There were two decisive moments of clarity, Epiphany moments where I really felt the presence and call of the Lord in my heart, when many of the doubts and worries at the time were put aside. The first was my experience on the diocesan pilgrimage to Lourdes as a helper, the second my participation in the World Youth Day in Paris, two events in the same year of 1997. My Parish Priest, Fr Martin Thompson, thought it a good idea for me to go to these events and he sponsored me: he was right!

It was in Lourdes that I personally felt the sense of the priest being a servant, as one who is dedicated to serve the people of God. One day, a pilgrim I was looking after said to me that I would make a good priest; I felt both embarrassed and humbled. Later on in the week I spent some time in prayer at the Grotto before the statue of Our Lady, and as I prayed I felt a real sense of serenity and peace, that the Lord was calling me and that he would be with me, sustaining me with His grace, if I said Yes to him. A month later I was in Paris for World Youth Day and seeing so many young Catholics living their faith with joy inspired me so much and gave me much hope. For me, seeing with fresh eyes that the Church was vibrant, alive and that she needed priests to play their part in bringing hope and love to the world was tremendously exciting. I was on a 'spiritual high'. In Paris I met young seminarians, novices and young priests. I went to talks and prayer meetings for vocations.

For the first time I didn't feel alone in my vocation – there were others like me who felt called, normal people from all sorts of backgrounds, cultures and contexts.

At the papal vigil and Mass at Longchamps racecourse, one and half million young people gathered, a most impressive sight! At the vigil, The Holy Father spoke about the subject of martyrdom, and cited the many examples of young people, many of whom were younger than me, who had given up their lives for Christ. He spoke about and we heard from persecuted Christians around the world, who today endure hardships and often death for practising their faith. It was powerful to hear; however what struck me was the question that the Pope posed to all of us which, as often was the case when Pope John Paul spoke, sounded as if he was personally addressing me! He asked the assembled mass, "What are you going to do for Christ in the new millennium?" It was a question that hit me hard. It was as if Pope John Paul knew what I was praying and discerning about over that year; I felt that the Holy Spirit through the words of the Holy Father had challenged me to make a decision.

After coming back from these two momentous events I had the courage and confidence to admit to my friends and family that I wanted to be a priest. This news was received warmly by my friends, in fact they were not surprised at all! My parents were fairly happy but they wanted me, I think, to consider university and a different career, to get some money – not an unreasonable expectation from one's parents with their own expectations and aspirations for their children, also we were not particularly well off!

I went and spoke to my Parish Priest who spoke to the bishop, who thought the same as my parents. Well at least about the university thing! I felt the spiritual bubble had been burst, but with a sense of calm and perspective I placed my trust in the Lord. After much prayer and reflection I thought university wouldn't be a bad thing, it would broaden my knowledge and experience, which I would bring to the priesthood. So I left for Cardiff University to study Law in September 1998.

I loved my time at university, but with that experience under my belt and after much reflection I would say that it could be a dangerous place for a vocation, in so far as it is a place where it can be severely tested. An aspiring vocation needs friendship, nurturing, support and advice. Fortunately I found this in the person of the university chaplain, who was a diocesan priest and very much a character. He taught me much and helped me get involved with the chaplaincy, where I met many other fellow Catholics. University is the place where many students, away from home and any pressures from parents, make the courageous decision to practise their faith of their own accord, and what struck me was how many good people there were who managed against any peer pressure to get down to Mass at the chaplaincy (mercifully Mass was on a Sunday evening!) The mutual support and friendship was important. I must admit that I found university a challenge, not necessarily the academic work, but the pressures on you to conform to what everyone else does: the drinking, partying and all that flows from that. For me, it was back to keeping my vocation a secret as I did not want people to know, since I thought they would treat me differently, and that my university experience might be severely damaged.

To discern a vocation in the milieu of studying hard

and partying hard was very difficult! People have different priorities and agendas, and the attraction and pull of many things which were not conducive to a vocation were strong. Parties, nightclubs, sex, drugs were all readily available and deemed the normal thing to do – how was I, an aspiring priest, to live amidst all these temptations and pressures? This is where faith and prayer, perseverance and fortitude are fundamental. To have good friends and confidantes is tremendously important too.

As I continued to discern my vocation at university, I began to sense some doubts as to whether I was holy and good enough to be a priest. I thought that I was too selfish, I wanted to do my own thing, on my part there was too much self-will. Why couldn't I do what everyone else did? However in moments various questions would keep coming back to me: what would make me happy? What did I really want to do, or rather what did God want me to do? I remembered that question that Pope John Paul II asked in Paris, I remembered the Grotto at Lourdes. I remembered the placement in the parish, I remembered the priests whom I admired. I remembered God calling me in all those events and through many people. I thought I could not ignore any longer these promptings from God.

Through the affirmation and encouragement of my Parish Priest and other priest friends, from both back home in Arundel and Brighton, but also the priests I got to know in Cardiff who helped me greatly, offering me Spiritual Direction and guidance, I decided in my third year at university to 'put out into the deep'. I came to realise that with God's grace, with his help, if it be his holy will, then I could be a priest – all I would have to do would be to offer myself and test my vocation formally.

I was accepted for the diocese as a student for the priesthood, and after various interviews and testing, Bishop Kieran Conry sent me to Rome for seven years. There I met so many wonderful people, many priests and seminarians whom I count as close friends. Friendship as I have mentioned is paramount in a priest's life, and indeed in an aspiring priest's life, for it is in friendship that a priest finds affirmation, support, serenity and love – primarily in a spiritual friendship with Christ, to whom the seminarian and priest seeks to grow closer, but also in human friendships, which will be indispensable later as you live out your priesthood.

Seminary often isn't the easiest of places to grow into a good and holy priest but it is the only opportunity to grow in pastoral charity; to grow in sanctity and wisdom; to become a man of prayer; to learn to preach, teach, govern, and to steward; to grow in affective maturity; to grow intellectually in the sacred sciences and other knowledge and ultimately to grow as a human being who is aspiring to become a celibate priest in the Catholic Church. For me it was often a challenging time: I made mistakes, I faced many challenges and trials (after all it isn't a holiday camp!) but I also experienced much happiness and many joys as I journeyed through formation. Seminary is a place where one should experience a growth in self-knowledge; as the primary agent of your formation, the Holy Spirit guides you with the help of your co-operation, openness and generosity, to be formed into a holy and devoted priest.

Many of your fellow seminarians may leave, and I found this sad. But you begin to look at your own vocation and ask anew "What is the Lord calling me to do?" It is in these moments I found myself re-affirming my commitment to the Lord.

I have been a happy and fulfilled priest serving God's people in Guildford since the day of my Ordination. Each day the Lord places wonderful people before me to minister to and to be able to offer Holy Mass is an awesome privilege. To be an *alter Christus* (another Christ) is to play a unique role in the work of salvation. To be Christ's eyes, ears, hands, mouth, his very body is a vocation that I encourage any man to consider, and for that man to place their trust and faith in wherever the Lord may ask him to go.

Benedict XVI concluded his message for the Day of Prayer for Vocations 2010 by observing that "in order to foster vocations to the ministerial priesthood and the consecrated life, and to be more effective in promoting the discernment of vocations, we cannot do without the example of those who have already said 'yes' to God and to his plan for the life of each individual."

"Personal witness," he specifies, "in the form of concrete existential choices, will encourage young people for their part to make demanding decisions affecting their future."

I hope and pray that I too can be an effective, joyful and authentic witness, just like the priests of my childhood and youth, so that others may see in me something worth offering their lives for as they ponder whether to say "yes" to the Lord.

A Military Chaplain in the Royal Air Force

Mgr JOHN WALSH

*Mgr John Walsh is a Chaplain in the RAF.
He was ordained priest for the Archdiocese
of Liverpool on 10 July 1983.*

I was born into a Catholic family, the first born of five children. Mine was a very ordinary family and the Faith was an integral part of our life. So among my earliest memories were times spent in prayer together, usually the Rosary, and Mass on Sunday. My earliest perception of a call to the priesthood came through the Mass. I was fascinated by the priest and his actions at the altar and so it was not surprising that I wanted to imitate what I saw. If you were to ask any priest whether he had 'rehearsed' the Mass as a young boy, you might be surprised at how many tell you that they did.

My memories of those early 'Masses' were not always pleasant however. On one occasion I destroyed a newly purchased bed sheet by cutting a hole in the middle of it to go over my head and drawing crosses all over it with a biro! The clip around my 'priestly' ear that followed made sure I was more cautious in the future! Throughout these early years, I was moving towards an attachment to, and love of, the Mass. It was only when I became an altar server at the age of nine that I really began to sense the presence of God, especially in the Blessed Sacrament. Those years were a time of great confusion in the Church, but our Parish Priest had a great love of the Mass and cultivated an atmosphere of reverence and prayerfulness.

As I moved into my teenage years I was thinking about possible careers. Most of my ideas centred around flying and travel in general. I was fascinated by the prospect of travelling to other countries and seeing other ways of life. But the idea of the priesthood remained strong and never went away. By the age of fifteen and shortly before leaving school, I had decided that I wanted to be a priest. Although I had been attracted to the priesthood from a young age, the final moment of decision took time. The crucial factor in my teenage years was my service at the altar. The insistence of my Parish Priest on an atmosphere of reverent silence in the church drew my attention more and more to the Tabernacle and to the One within. I remember asking Our Lord for a 'sign' that this is what he wanted me to do, but no sign came. Instead, over time, there was a growing conviction that this is what he wanted. The conviction became clearer when I prayed, when I made time to enter into conversation with God. Such conversations were always simple, but through them I gradually began to understand that it was not a question of what I wanted, but of what God was asking of me.

At the age of sixteen I entered the Junior Seminary at Upholland, now long since closed. It was an important moment for me. Even though I attended a Catholic school, I did not find sympathy when I spoke of my attraction to the priesthood. There were lonely moments and little support. When I arrived at seminary I found myself among young men of my own age who also believed that God was calling them to be priests. It was my first experience of 'fraternity' and one which became increasingly important over the years that followed. It is for this reason that I am convinced that those who are drawn to the priesthood should regularly spend time with each other to find the necessary support, encouragement and formation. I was only able to take the first step on the road to the priesthood because of my Parish Priest and Vocations Director. As I look back now, I am deeply grateful to both men for their example and encouragement.

The period of formation required for priesthood is long and demanding. It would take eight years of seminary life, studies and formation before the day of my priestly ordination arrived. It is very difficult to put into words the sentiments and deepest feelings of that day. After all, it was the fulfilment of a call I had sensed many years before as a young boy. But I would say that a deep sense of the love of God was the clearest memory of the day and a deep joy in the company of my parents, brothers and sisters and brother priests.

The memory of that day always stays with me. It has remained vivid. The years that have followed since that day have taken me through many varied experiences in many places. I ministered in a number of parishes in and around Liverpool, including chaplaincy work in hospitals and schools. After a time, the novelty of being a priest begins to fade. I remembered the words of an elderly priest to me just before my priestly ordination: "keep it fresh!" I soon realised that the priestly ministry had to be renewed and refreshed. I did not want to become dull, stale or miserable. I was aware that people expected their priests to be joyful, convinced of their calling and happy to serve. The powerful personal example of Pope John Paul II was a great influence on me. His vigour, joyfulness and deep faith was a constant source of inspiration. Even though he had been called to serve the Church as the Successor of Peter, it was his identity as a priest that continued to move and inspire him.

In 2003 I sought the permission of my Bishop to enter the Royal Air Force as a chaplain. I was reminded recently of the words of the Holy Father that when we give our lives to God, he takes nothing away from us but gives much in return. It seems that God has fulfilled some of those early boyhood dreams of flying and travel to different countries. What I could not have foreseen as a boy was the way in which God would use my priestly ministry to touch the hearts of those searching for him, even on the flight deck of a large transport plane flying to the Middle East.

As the padre of their particular squadron, the crew of this aircraft had invited me to join them for a seven day mission to Cyprus and Bahrain, accompanying two fast jets that needed to be regularly refuelled in mid-air. The flight to Cyprus went well, but the second leg of the journey was problematic. We were delayed in Cyprus for two days because of problems with flight clearances. This meant a change of plan and a new route. It was providential. We flew over the Sinai desert with a clear view of Mount Sinai and the Red Sea, an area rich in biblical history. Some of the crew remembered their school lessons and asked me to explain the stories again. I remember the silent interest as I recounted the story of the Exodus from Egypt and the journey of the people of Israel to the Promised Land. To see the place where all of this had happened spread out before us was moving. But it seemed that one of the crew was more moved than I was. Later that evening, after we had arrived at our destination, he approached me quietly when he was sure the others could not see him, and asked me to explain more about the Scriptures and the faith of the Church. Some time later I had the joy of receiving him into the Church. It all began with a simple explanation of a story from the Bible.

My years as a military chaplain have seen other occasions similar to that one; quiet conversations, months spent in the desert close to conflict, much laughter, and frequent surprise at the courage and goodness of those faced with great adversity. Our Lord promised his disciples that all who had left family, home and much else behind them would be rewarded not just in eternity but also in this life. This has been my experience. When a priest realises that there is nothing more beautiful or more necessary than the salvation of souls, then the joy of working for souls and loving souls is a very great reward. To lead souls to God and to salvation is the very heart of the ministry of the priest, whether in a parish, a hospital, a school or on the flight deck of a transport aircraft. This is the great joy of the Catholic priesthood: that wherever we are, we are priests first and foremost, men consecrated for the salvation of souls.

In common with all human beings, priests have good days and difficult days. Sacrifice is an essential part of the Christian vocation no matter what our calling. But the priest must stand particularly close to the Cross. Frequent prayer, especially the Rosary, and frequent Confession helps the priest to remain steadfast. The world in which we minister as priests will seek to convince us that the Cross is not necessary and that 'self fulfilment' and 'ease' are a fitting reward for those who have 'given up' so much. It is of course a lie. When we are tempted to believe it, then we experience great unhappiness.

I reflected on the importance of the Mass in my life as a boy and a teenager at the beginning of this article. I shall end by speaking of the Mass with the hindsight of twenty seven years as a priest.

The priest is asked to stand close to the Cross because, with his own hands, he renews the Sacrifice of Calvary day in and day out for the salvation of souls. It is because of Calvary that he can absolve sin in the name of the Crucified One. Any man who is considering a call to the priesthood must understand that the priest finds his identity and fulfilment in the Holy Mass and that a love of the Mass is not just preferable but essential. Some might find this a rather 'narrow' understanding of the priesthood, but it is liberating to reflect that it is not our personality or gifts and abilities that our people need. If that were the case, many of us would have fallen over long ago. It is the Mass and the Sacraments they need and only the priest can provide them. Some might find this overwhelming, but we are never alone. Our Lady stands next to us at the foot of the Cross. With few words but much love, she will reassure, guide and protect us. This is why a constant deepening of faith is necessary for all Christians, but particularly those who are called to the priesthood.

If you are reading this account because you are considering the priesthood, then know that it is a wonderful, joyful life and that I would happily live through it all again. Whatever your plans or dreams remember this, that there is only one question that needs to be answered: what does God want of me? Seek the answer to that question and you will find great happiness.